HIDDEN TREASURES

RENFREWSHIRE

Edited by Allison Dowse

First published in Great Britain in 2002 by
YOUNG WRITERS
Remus House,
Coltsfoot Drive,
Peterborough, PE2 9JX
Telephone (01733) 890066

HB ISBN 0 75433 830 4
SB ISBN 0 75433 831 2

FOREWORD

This year, the Young Writers' Hidden Treasures competition proudly presents a showcase of the best poetic talent from over 72,000 up-and-coming writers nationwide.

Young Writers was established in 1991 and we are still successful, even in today's technologically-led world, in promoting and encouraging the reading and writing of poetry.

The thought, effort, imagination and hard work put into each poem impressed us all, and once again, the task of selecting poems was a difficult one, but nevertheless, an enjoyable experience.

We hope you are as pleased as we are with the final selection and that you and your family continue to be entertained with *Hidden Treasures Renfrewshire* for many years to come.

CONTENTS

Brediland Primary School

Ross Thomson	15
Emma Pullar	16
Ryan Wereski	16
Alan Forsyth	17
Jemma Markie	18
Benjamin Crawford	18
Fraser Coyle	19
Siobhan Kelly	20
Riada McCredie	21
Ryan MacDonald	22
Conor Paterson	22
Tracy Gibson	23
Greg Dribbell	23
Hayley Gilchrist	24
Lorna Jack	24
Jordan Hughes	25
Nur Hemsi	26
Amanda Howie	26

Bridge of Weir Primary School

Kirsty Sanders	27
Mark Thompson	27
Linzi Gordon	27
Robert Paton	28
Craig Chamberlain	28
Sarah Thomson	29
Christopher Mackie	29
Tom Kelly	30
Amanda Maxwell	30
Matthew Bristow	30
Michael Hardie	31
Vhari Toole	31
Sandie Macdonald	32
Rebecca Cunningham	32
Louise Andrew	32
Fiona Meldrum	33
Kerri Hunter	33

Lynne Mckenzie	34
Scott Mckenzie	34
Hannah Wright	34
Christopher Murphy	35
Laura Barney	35
Rachael Ferguson	36
Carol Hunter	36
Paul Stewart	36
Connor Stevenson	37
Caroline Finlay	37
Michael Bell	38
Adam Rushton	38
Gary McCrossan	39
Colin Guthrie	39

Craigielea Primary School

Ryan Muldoon	40
Kerry Ritchie	41
Robert Hamilton	41
Lisa Thomas	42
Craig Whitelaw	42
Tracey Hammond	43
Anne McCabe	44
Leon Morrow	44
Jamie Evans	45
Jordan Bruce	45

Ferguslie Primary School

Darren McGregor	46
Nicole Cameron	46
Amanda Walls	46

Gallowhill Primary School

Robert Hulley	47
Christopher Hamilton	47
Heather Corbett	48
Graeme MacPherson	48
John Currie	49

Stewart White	49
Nicola Archibald	50
Leigh-Anne Reddick	50
Raymond Paul	51
Mark McNicholl	52
Laura Benson	52
Seumais Peter Simpson	53
Nicole Andrews	54
Stephanie Stewart	54
Linzi Hanratty	55
Stephanie Cooney	56
Kerrys Stevenson	56
Danielle McMeekin	57
Stacey Moyes	57
Danielle Gallacher	58
Simone Footitt	58
Kieron McLardie	59
Ryan Love	59
Kim Black	60
Gary Dean	61
Lauren Swanson	62
Thomas Wright	62
Christina Rankin	63
Clair Lochrie	64
Scott McPherson	64

Highholm Primary School

Ruaridh Hamilton	65
Laura Hamilton	66
Elizabeth McKay	66
Gareth Lindsay	67
Jamie McLeod	68
Graeme Hendry	68
Emma Stoddart	69
Ailsa Craynor	70
Siobhan Hendry	70
Matthew Carnegie	71
Carrie Gallacher	72

Ryan Kane	72
Craig Hill	73
Ryan Cheshire	74
Martyn Wotherspoon	74
Kerry Thompson	75
Sara Knox	76
Amy Laura Woodcock	76
Jonathan Ferguson	77
Thomas Wilson	78

Houston Primary School

Jennifer Priestley	79
Christina Bardell	79
Jessica Maskrey	80
Ben Chapman	80
Ellen Robinson	81
Emma Hollinsworth	81
Grier McDonald Porch	82
Douglas Holmes	82
Stuart Black	83
Blair Meikle	83
Kirsty Horn	84
David Greig	84
Julie Richmond	85
Craig Howie	85
Kirsty Murray	86
Ryan McMaster	86
Gemma Robertson	87
Scott Whyte	87
Cara Drummond	88
Emma Whyte	88
Katy Richardson	89
Lee Adam	89
Heather Kirkland	90
Alastair Griffiths	90
Ryan Blair	91
Rebecca McCluskie	91
Lindsay McLellan	92

Cameron Sim	92
Murray Noble	93
Adam MacAlister	93
Jack Doak	94
Fiona Hunter	94
Grant Rankin	95
Craig McCowan	95
Nadine Graham	96
Finlay Fraser	96
Scott Campbell	97
Kirsty Smith	97
Alex Cameron	98
Calum Jowett	99
Jacolyn Kincaid	99
Kathryn Lindsay	100
Steven Kerr	100
Robyn Martin	101
Brian Stephen	101
Georgia Porch	102
Emma Calvert	102
Gregor Preston-Jones	103
Rachel Harris	103
Andrew Morrison	104
Fraser Jowett	104
Craig McKissack	104
Liam Hunter	105
Lauren McCrudden	105
Craig Hawthorn	105
Douglas Webb	106
Sam Jamieson	106
Rebecca Robertson	106
Abdul Tarmal	107
Kirsty Clark	107
Katie Whittle	107
Naveed Rasul	108
Sarah Lyall	108
Iona Lee	109
Samantha Murray	109

Kilbarchan Primary School

Alan McLean	109
Lorne Campbell	110
Jordan Clark	110
Lindsey Anderson	111
Nicole Brown	111
Lynsey Macleod	112
Helen Tatner	112
Jordan Walker	113
Laura McCracken	113
Darren Andrew	114
Laura Ross	114
Grant Marshall	115
Katryn Stuart	115
Lauren Hyndman	116
Sarah Dyer	116
Christine Cameron	117
Ryan McKellar	118
Elspeth Chalmers	118
Lauren White	119
Hollie Porteous	120
Mark Docherty	120
David Seymour	121

Langbank Primary School

Victoria Smith	121
Callum MacRae	122
Tom Ellis	123
Duncan Fletcher	124
Simon Beveridge	125
Daniel Keegan	126
Laura Mitchell	127
Emma Gilchrist	128
Samantha Campbell	129
Bruce Abernethy	130
Jacqueline Hamilton	130
Suzy Hansen	131
Charlotte Linn	131

Frazer Macdonald	147
Stuart Caldwell	148
Ashleigh McMichael	148
Daniella Gallacher	149
Amanda Craig	149
Charlotte Taylor	150
Rachael Pringle	150
Michael McMaster	151
James Campbell	151
Lauren Coyle	152
Nicole Wilson	152
Kieran Whiteford	152
Sean Kelly	153
Craig Mackenzie	153
Christopher McShane	153
Mark Wyllie	154
Sarah Chalk	154
David Sloan	155
Kirsty Kent	155
Christopher Logan	155
Lee Jones	156

Rashielea Primary School

Melanie McMaster	156
Abbie Rose Shepherd	157
Siobhan McHugh	157
Hayley Walsh	158
Jordan Scott	158
Emily Smith	158
Megan McLellan	159
Matthew Ferguson	159
Robyn Jade Agnew	159
Stephanie Murtagh	160
Martin Hughes	160
Steven Andrew Boyd	161
Emma Mackay	161
Rebecca Cottis	162
Ross Donaldson	162

The Poems

MY EYES

My eyes are brown,
Brown as chocolate melting
In the hot summer's sun.
Brown as squelching muck
After the winter's rain.
Brown as a muffin baked in the oven,
My eyes are brown.

Christopher Gibson (9)
Arkleston Primary School

MY EYES

My eyes are brown
Brown as the chocolate I like to eat
Brown as crunching leaves I like to stand on
Brown as a log I like to walk on
My eyes are brown.

Rachel Lindsay (8)
Arkleston Primary School

MY EYES

My eyes are blue
Blue as a dolphin diving in the sea
Blue as the sky after the rain
Blue as a glittery gel pen
My eyes are blue.

Gulnaaz Hamid (8)
Arkleston Primary School

MY EYES

My eyes are green
Green as the grass after a summer shower
Green as an emerald sparkling in a dark, misty fog
Green as the seaweed drifting at the bottom of the sea
My eyes are green.

Rebecca Stevenson (8)
Arkleston Primary School

MY EYES

My eyes are blue
Blue as a sapphire sparkling in a ring
Blue as a bluebird in the sky
Blue as the gentle sea on a summer's day
My eyes are blue.

Charlie Kennedy (8)
Arkleston Primary School

MY EYES

My eyes are blue
Blue as sapphires shining in the sun
Blue as our jumpers blowing in the wind
Blue as the ocean splashing in the sun
My eyes are blue.

Stephen Hay (8)
Arkleston Primary School

MY EYES

My eyes are blue
Blue as the sun glittering on a blue gel pen
Blue are the sparkling ocean on a hot summer's day,
Blue as the school jumpers we wear
My eyes are blue.

Ryan Alexander (8)
Arkleston Primary School

MY EYES

My eyes are blue
Blue as a bluebell growing in the forest
Blue as the sea on a hot summer's day
Blue as a gel pen glittering in the sun.
My eyes are blue.

Lee Thomas (8)
Arkleston Primary School

MY EYES

My eyes are brown
Brown as a coconut hanging from a palm tree
Brown as a lovely chocolate bar, waiting to be eaten
Brown as mud, waiting to be stood in.
My eyes are brown.

Craig McLauchlan (8)
Arkleston Primary School

MY EYES

My eyes are green
Green as the grass after
rain on the hills,
Green as the cabbage on my plate
waiting to be eaten,
Green as the emerald
sparkling on my mum's finger.
My eyes are green.

Rebecca Orr (7)
Arkleston Primary School

MY EYES

My eyes are grey
Grey as the fog on a foggy day
Grey as a dolphin leaping in the sea
Grey as the ground on a wet day
My eyes are grey.

Dylan Connor (8)
Arkleston Primary School

MY EYES

My eyes are blue
Blue as a dolphin sparkling in the sunshine
Blue as bubblegum bursting in the air
Blue as the sea swaying on a summer's day.

Emma Wylie (8)
Arkleston Primary School

MY EYES

My eyes are brown
Brown as my fat dog Mindy
Brown as a coconut shell which I like to crack
Brown as my toast which I eat in the morning,
My eyes are brown.

Rachael Devlin (8)
Arkleston Primary School

DISAPPOINTMENT

Disappointment was when I went to hire Toy Story Racer
but all the copies were out.
Disappointment was when I was to go to Spain but it was cancelled.
Disappointment was when I was told to go to the doctor's and instead
I wanted to play outside.
Disappointment was when I had to go to my gran's house
and there was nothing to do.
Disappointment was when I was going to a football match
and it was called off.
Disappointment was when I was going canoeing and they
ran out of boats.
Disappointment was when I was going to my friend's and then
I was going to my gran's.
Disappointment was when I wanted to go out to play
but I had to do my homework.
Disappointment was when I was going swimming and it was closed.
Disappointment was when I was going to see Shrek but I could
not go because I was not feeling well.

Adam Bell (9)
Bargarran Primary School

DISAPPOINTMENT

Disappointment is going on holiday and it was cancelled for one day.
Disappointment is having to go to school and not playing football.
Disappointment is if I was having a sleepover and then my mum
said 'No!'
Disappointment is wanting to see 'Harry Potter' but not going.
Disappointment is when I was getting ready to go to football but
it was cancelled.
Disappointment is if I wanted to rent a video and my mum said 'No!'
Disappointment is when I have to tidy my room instead of
playing football.
Disappointment is if my little sister trashes the place and I have to
tidy up.
Disappointment is when I have to go shopping with my mum.
Disappointment is when I was going to see 'Cats & Dogs' but
we didn't go.

Craig McInnes (9)
Bargarran Primary School

DISAPPOINTMENT

Disappointment is being promised to see Shrek but then not going.
Disappointment is when your holiday flight is delayed for three hours.
Disappointment is when you have to go shopping.
Disappointment is doing homework before playing outside.
Disappointment is being promised to go bowling, but not going.
Disappointment is having to go to school.
Disappointment is renting a video, when there's none left.
Disappointment is wanting a packet of smell pens, but only
receiving one.
Disappointment is when I have to get up really early.
Disappointment is when I want to go outside, but I can't.

David McCallum (9)
Bargarran Primary School

DISAPPOINTMENT

Disappointment is when I was supposed to be going to a pantomime
but my brothers went instead.
Disappointment is having to do homework before playing outside.
Disappointment is a member of the family dying before a
special occasion.
Disappointment is having to go shopping with my brothers.
Disappointment is having to go to the dentist to get a tooth pulled out.
Disappointment is when I'm late coming home at night and I have to
get up early in the morning.
Disappointment is going to school to do work.
Disappointment is hurting myself and having to go to the hospital.
Disappointment is tidying my room when it's messy.
Disappointment is helping my mum decorate the living room.

Heather Gibson (9)
Bargarran Primary School

DISAPPOINTMENT

Disappointment is when my brother split up with his wife.
Disappointment is when you want to hire a video but none are there.
Disappointment is not being allowed to do something you
really want to.
Disappointment is when your holidays are cancelled.
Disappointment is falling out with your best friend.
Disappointment is when you get extra homework.
Disappointment is being invited to a sleepover but your mum
says 'No!'
Disappointment is when I was a baby, I only saw my dad at weekends.
Disappointment is having to wait for ages to get into the pool.
Disappointment is having no one to play with.

Sophie MacConnachie (9)
Bargarran Primary School

DISAPPOINTMENT

Disappointment is Mum and Dad promising to go bowling,
but we don't go.
Disappointment is having to do homework before going out to play.
Disappointment is wanting a video but Mum says 'No!'
Disappointment is hurting my knee and nearly not going
to Girl's Brigade.
Disappointment is not staying at my mum's friend's house in Aberdeen.
Disappointment is not being allowed to buy the Harry Potter
set of books.
Disappointment is wanting one PC game and one PlayStation game
and not being allowed either.
Disappointment is not going to my friend's house to play.
Disappointment is not being allowed to have my friends over
for a sleepover.
Disappointment is having wee cousin Blair staying overnight.

Jenna McKay (9)
Bargarran Primary School

DISAPPOINTMENT

Disappointment is booking up for Florida and then the holiday
is cancelled.
Disappointment is going to school and not messing around at home.
Disappointment is being promised something and you don't get to do it.
Disappointment is coming second in a race, about one second after
the first person.
Disappointment is when you lose your money and you can't find it.
Disappointment is when you have to do homework.
Disappointment is being told to work and you can't do something else.
Disappointment is when you finish something on time.
Disappointment is when you can't do something again which you liked.

Scott MacKay (8)
Bargarran Primary School

DISAPPOINTMENT

Disappointment was when I wanted to go to my friend's house
to climb up trees but I couldn't.
Disappointment was when me and my friends wanted to go swimming
but it was closed.
Disappointment is when I go home and have to do my homework
before I can watch TV.
Disappointment was when my mum and dad broke up,
I could only see my dad every second week.
Disappointment was when I had to wear a dress because it was
my gran's birthday and my gran was not wearing a dress.
Disappointment is when I am doing a jigsaw and my brother wrecks it.
Disappointment was when I had to tidy my room.
Disappointment was when I asked my mum to get some new hair-bands
and she didn't.
Disappointment was when I wanted to go to Koko's but I couldn't.

Kirsty Jane Marquis (9)
Bargarran Primary School

DISAPPOINTMENT

Disappointment is if I'm told to do my homework and
I want to go out to play.
Disappointment is visiting the shops with my mum.
Disappointment is having to eat mushroom soup.
Disappointment is when my granda died.
Disappointment is waiting for ages before the plane which
I was supposed to be catching, was delayed.
Disappointment is when I wanted to play the computer
but it wasn't working properly.
Disappointment is when it's the end of the weekend.
Disappointment is when I have to get up in the morning.

Laura Kerr (8)
Bargarran Primary School

DISAPPOINTMENT

Disappointment was being asked if I wanted to go swimming
                                    which was then cancelled.
Disappointment was wanting to hire a video, but someone else had it.
Disappointment was when Mum said we could go to Perth,
                                    but we weren't good enough.
Disappointment was when my grandpa died.
Disappointment was when the school holidays finished.
Disappointment was when I was getting ready to go out to play
                                    but it started raining.
Disappointment was when I went to the library which was closed.
Disappointment was when I wasn't allowed to stay overnight
                                    at my friend's.
Disappointment was when I wasn't allowed to get a PlayStation game.

Kirstie Ann Smith (9)
Bargarran Primary School

DISAPPOINTMENT

Disappointment is getting my laptop two weeks late.
Disappointment is doing homework before going out to play.
Disappointment is getting my new bed for my new bedroom a day late.
Disappointment is being promised to see Shrek and not going.
Disappointment is wanting a puppy and getting a kitten.
Disappointment is when my mum tells me to tidy my room.
Disappointment is wanting my swimming pool out and
                                    not being allowed.
Disappointment is wanting to visit friends and it being cancelled.
Disappointment is being promised to be picked up at five o'clock
                                    but being picked up at six.
Disappointment is wanting to go to the park and going to
                                    the pictures instead.

Eilish Smith (9)
Bargarran Primary School

DISAPPOINTMENT

Disappointment was when my mum promised me that we would go
and see my uncle who lives in London but we didn't go.
Disappointment was when my mum said we would go and see Grease
but we didn't go.
Disappointment is when my friend is not allowed to come out
to play with me.
Disappointment is when I'm not allowed to go out to play
before doing my homework.
Disappointment is when I have to tidy my room.
Disappointment was when my sister messed up my room and
I got the blame.
Disappointment is when I'm not allowed something to eat
before my dinner.
Disappointment is when I need to clean out my rabbits.
Disappointment is when I'm not allowed to go swimming
with my friends.
Disappointment is when I have a sore tummy and I can't eat any sweets.

Hayley Bolton (9)
Bargarran Primary School

DISAPPOINTMENT

Disappointment was when I couldn't get a hamster.
Disappointment was when my brother said he would take me
to the cinema but he didn't.
Disappointment is when I have to go to the shops.
Disappointment is when my mum says I can't have TV at night.
Disappointment is when I can't go to karate.
Disappointment is when I have to stay in.
Disappointment was when I couldn't make something for my gran.
Disappointment is when my mum says I have to do my reading.
Disappointment is when I have to go to my bedroom.

Holly Brown (9)
Bargarran Primary School

DISAPPOINTMENT

Disappointment was when I was promised to go and see Cats & Dogs
but I was cheeky and didn't get to go.
Disappointment is having to do your homework when you want
to go out and play.
Disappointment is having to go and look at new cars, then listen
to prices but you want to go swimming.
Disappointment was when my dad said I could have a friend to stay
but mum said no.
Disappointment is having to eat fish when my favourite meal is
in the freezer.
Disappointment is having to do the garden, like cutting the grass
when I could be watching my favourite programme.
Disappointment is when I have to clean my rabbit's cage.
Disappointment is when I have to put away my ironing.

Kirstie E Smith (9)
Bargarran Primary School

DISAPPOINTMENT

Disappointment is doing homework before going out to play.
Disappointment is wanting to hire a video but finding it isn't there.
Disappointment is wanting to go swimming or ice-skating
but it's cancelled.
Disappointment is going to the cinema with a friend but finding
the cinema is closed.
Disappointment is wanting to stay over at a friend's but my mum
saying no.
Disappointment is wanting to go to Braehead but finding it is closed.
Disappointment is me being ill and having to stay off school.
Disappointment is watching TV but having to go and wash dishes.

Lisa Cresswell (9)
Bargarran Primary School

DISAPPOINTMENT

Disappointment was when I was going to George Square ice rink
but it had been taken down.
Disappointment was when Robyn never came to play for two weeks.
Disappointment was when I wanted to find a book,
but I must have lost it.
Disappointment was when I got into trouble for not eating my dinner.
Disappointment was when I was sick at Christmas.
Disappointment is because my dad still hasn't got batteries
for Twitcher.
Disappointment was when I had to stay home from school
because I was ill.
Disappointment was when my brother had to go to hospital.
Disappointment was when I got told to turn the computer down.
Disappointment was when I got told to eat my dinner
when I was full up.

Ashleigh Wiseman (9)
Bargarran Primary School

DISAPPOINTMENT

Disappointment is not getting special treats.
Disappointment is not being allowed to see a movie.
Disappointment is tidying up my room instead of doing something else.
Disappointment is eating food I don't like to eat.
Disappointment is not being allowed to go out.
Disappointment is washing dishes when I don't want to.
Disappointment is going somewhere I don't want to.
Disappointment is not getting any pocket money.
Disappointment is not visiting friends.
Disappointment is when you have to go shopping.

Craig Smith (9)
Bargarran Primary School

DISAPPOINTMENT

Disappointment was when my mum said my friend could stay
                                        and she has not.
Disappointment was doing homework before going out to play.
Disappointment was when my holiday flight was three hours late.
Disappointment was when my mum said she would take me
                                        ice-skating but she did not.
Disappointment is when you cannot get something on the Web.
Disappointment is when I cannot find something.
Disappointment is going to hire a video and finding there are none left.
Disappointment is when my mum tells me to tidy my room
                                        instead of me going out to play.
Disappointment is when I have to get up in the morning for school.
Disappointment is when I cannot go up to my gran's.

Lauren McAndrew (8)
Bargarran Primary School

DISAPPOINTMENT

Disappointment was when I was grounded for a week.
Disappointment was when I wanted smelly pens and I only got one.
Disappointment was when I wanted to go to Ireland but I was
                                        not allowed to go.
Disappointment was when my little cousin got more sweets than me.
Disappointment was when I had to go out when I didn't want to.
Disappointment was when I was getting stitches,
                                        I had to stay off school.
Disappointment was when I had to do the dishes.
Disappointment was when I got sent to my room.
Disappointment was when my mum lied to me about
                                        having somebody overnight.
Disappointment was when my mum never let me on the computer.

Neil Boyle (9)
Bargarran Primary School

DISAPPOINTMENT

Disappointment is when my sister gets me into trouble.
Disappointment is when I have to unload my dishwasher.
Disappointment is when I have to do my homework.
Disappointment is when I have to tidy up my room.
Disappointment is when I have to go shopping.
Disappointment is when my flight is cancelled.
Disappointment is when I want some new pens.
Disappointment is when my sister promises
                to take me somewhere and doesn't.
Disappointment is when I have to go to bed.
Disappointment is when I have to tidy up my living room.

Stephanie Renwick (9)
Bargarran Primary School

HIDDEN TREASURE

H   idden under the sea
I   n the stormy weather
D   own in a chest
D   eep, deep down
E   meralds and jewels
N   umerous people look for it

T   here's an octopus lying waiting
R   eady for someone to steal the treasure
E   ventually someone tries
A   ttacked by the octopus
S   oon it will be over
U   nder the water where no one can escape
R   eturn no more to get the treasure
E   nd has come the octopus has guarded it well.

Ross Thomson (10)
Brediland Primary School

MY SEASONS RENGA

Spring

A lot of sunshine
There is a cool breeze in spring
Cute babies are born

Summer

It's very hot in summer
We have lots of water fights
Ice lollies we eat

Autumn

Now leaves fall from trees
Always falling to the ground
Branches are so bare

Winter

It's cold in the snow
Sledging down the hill is fun
Snowball fights are fun.

Emma Pullar (9)
Brediland Primary School

HIDDEN TREASURE

Down, down we go, under the sea,
I'm alone, it is just me,
Ready for adventure at any time,
I hope the treasure will be all mine,
Now I can see an old wooden chest,

What is in it can only be guessed,
But when I open it, inside is gold,
It could be over a thousand years old,
Amethysts and a huge jewel,
This is what I call cool!

Ryan Wereski (10)
Brediland Primary School

MY SEASONS RENGA

Spring

A lot of sunshine
There is a cool breeze in spring
Flowers grow in spring

Summer

I'm going to Spain
For my summer holiday
Summer is the best

Autumn

Leaves fall off the trees
It's very cold in autumn
Branches are so bare

Winter

It's cold in the snow
Sledging down the hills is fun
Skating on the ice.

Alan Forsyth (9)
Brediland Primary School

MY SEASONS RENGA

Winter

As the days go by
Have lots of fun in the snow
Snowflakes are falling

Autumn

Leaves fall from the trees
Leaves crunching under your feet
Standing in the leaves

Summer

Sunshine in the sky
I have lots of fun with you
Standing in the sun

Spring

Baby animals
Snowdrops now begin to grow
Animals are born.

Jemma Markie (9)
Brediland Primary School

HIDDEN TREASURE

Down we go into the mine,
People begin to moan and whine.
Rubies, sapphires, emeralds, gold,
Maybe even a thousand years old.
Wow, a diamond the size of a car,

We try to take it, but we don't get far.
There's a rumble, a bump and an enormous crack,
Suddenly everything goes dark,
Then I find myself in a dragon's lair,
Oh no, not another nasty nightmare.

Benjamin Crawford (10)
Brediland Primary School

MY SEASONS RENGA

Spring

Leaves are growing back
Another season is near
Time to go to school

Summer

It is hot again
Time to go outside and play
Time to go swimming

Autumn

Now it is autumn
The leaves are changing colours
And it is colder

Winter

The snow is coming
Time to play in the puddles
Christmas is quite near.

Fraser Coyle (9)
Brediland Primary School

A-Z OF HIDDEN TREASURE

A mazing amethysts
B eautiful blue topaz
C ool crystals
D azzling diamonds
E legant emeralds
F abulous friends
G orgeous garnets
H ilarious happiness
I rresistible ivory
J umping joy
K indness all around
L ovely lights
M arvellous money
N ice necklaces
O pulent opals
P erfect pearls
Q ueen's crown
R ich red rubies
S ilver stones
T alents that have been hidden
U nder the sand
V ery valuable
W elcoming me
eX tremely happy
Y ou would like this
Z illions and zillions of treasures in the chest.

Siobhan Kelly (10)
Brediland Primary School

HIDDEN TREASURE

Scuba-diving in the sea
Floating treasure chest coming towards me
I pull it up to the beach
Amazed to find

A ll this treasure just for me
B eautiful blue topaz
C oins of gold, silver and bronze
D azzling diamonds
E legant emeralds
F abulous fortunes
G littering gold
H undreds of hidden treasures
I like all this treasure - it's so great
J ewels and jewellery sparkling in the light
K ingly jewels
L ovely little crystals sitting in a box
M arvellous money
N ice things everywhere
O h such lovely opals
P retty little pearls
Q ueen's crowns
R eally nice rubies
S pecial rings
T errific tiaras
U nbelievably beautiful sapphires and garnets
V aluable amethysts
W onderful silver
eX tremely large chest
Y ellow diamonds
Z illions of treasure!

Riada McCredie (10)
Brediland Primary School

My Seasons Renga

Spring

Animals are born
Plants grow higher than ever
Bunnies are hopping

Summer

Sunshine is so warm
Roaring waves hit off the rocks
Seashells on the shore

Autumn

The wind is so strong
Leaves are falling - red, green, brown
Birds fly to warm ground

Winter

Freezing in the snow
Icicles hanging on trees
Making different shapes.

Ryan MacDonald (9)
Brediland Primary School

Hidden Treasure

H idden treasure in a dark, dark cave
I   found it there in the dark, dark cave
D eep, deep down
D own under the sea
E nough treasure to make me rich
N ow I can buy a football pitch.

Conor Paterson (10)
Brediland Primary School

MY SEASONS RENGA

Spring

Green grass all around
Babies are born in the spring
A lot of sunshine

Summer

It is very hot
Always eating ice lollies
Summer is the best

Autumn

Bare trees everywhere
Leaves are falling off the trees
It is very cold

Winter

Winter is snowy
No leaves on trees in winter
Skating on the ice.

Tracy Gibson (9)
Brediland Primary School

HIDDEN TREASURE

H idden on the deserted island
I n the middle of nowhere
D eep in the island
D own a hole
E meralds, rubies and huge, golden eggs
N ow it is mine.

Greg Dribbell (10)
Brediland Primary School

HIDDEN TREASURE

H   undreds of golden treasures
I   n a deep, dark cave
D   eep inside the deep, dark cave
D   ragons sleep
E   verywhere they lie
N   obody knows where the treasure is

T   reasure everywhere
R   ubies, crystals and pearls too
E   verywhere they are
A   nd there is a lot of it too
S   ilver and gold all over the place
U   nder and over things
R   eally nice
E   verywhere it is.

Hayley Gilchrist (10)
Brediland Primary School

MY SEASONS RENGA

Spring

Green grass all around
Babies are born in the spring
A cool breeze in spring

Summer

It's warm in summer
Summer is for water fights
I like the summer

Autumn

Leaves fall from the trees
It's very cold in autumn
Branches are so bare

Winter

It's cold in the air
Icicles hang down from roofs
Snow lies all around.

Lorna Jack (9)
Brediland Primary School

HIDDEN TREASURE

H   idden
I   n deep water
D   own, down
D   eep
E   meralds, jewels and silver
N   ever to be seen by anyone.

T   reasure chest
R   eal gold
E   meralds round the chest
A   methysts
S   hipwrecked Armada
U   nderneath the sea
R   eal gold and silver
E   very jewel shining brightly.

Jordan Hughes (10)
Brediland Primary School

HIDDEN TREASURE

H idden under the sand,
I   mpossible, is this really happening?
D iamonds, rubies, pearls and emeralds,
D azzling and dashing,
E ndlessly sparkling,
N odding up and down - wow!

T ell somebody, share the good news,
R un to find someone to tell,
E ager to take it to the museum,
A bsolutely great feelings running through me,
S howing off to hundreds of people,
U plifted and excited,
R eady to show my parents,
E verybody is shaking my hand.

Nur Hemsi (10)
Brediland Primary School

HIDDEN TREASURE

Under the sea there's treasure for me,
Treasure for me and my family,
Corrina and me scuba-diving in the sea.

We found the treasure and took it to the shore,
As we opened the chest, out popped more and more,
Crystals and diamonds for us to explore.

Once summer holidays are over,
I'll tell my friends about the never-ending treasure,
And for the rest of my life I can live in leisure,
No difficulty and annoyance, just a life of pleasure.

Amanda Howie (10)
Brediland Primary School

THE YACHT

The yacht
The clean yacht
The clean, white yacht
The clean, white yacht sailed
The clean, white yacht quickly sailed
The clean, white yacht quickly sailed across the ocean
The clean, white yacht quickly sailed across the bumpy, wavy ocean.

Kirsty Sanders (10)
Bridge of Weir Primary School

THE STEGOSAURUS

The stegosaurus
The vicious stegosaurus
The vicious stegosaurus ate
The vicious stegosaurus greedily ate
The vicious stegosaurus greedily ate a small plant
The vicious stegosaurus greedily ate a small, tasty plant.

Mark Thompson (10)
Bridge of Weir Primary School

THE ELF

The elf
The friendly elf
The friendly, cute elf smiled nicely
The friendly, cute elf smiled nicely at the girl
The friendly, cute elf smiled nicely at the little girl
The friendly, cute elf smiled nicely at the little, happy girl.

Linzi Gordon (10)
Bridge of Weir Primary School

KIWI

I saw a plump kiwi bird
Hiding in the grass
Its crazy facial features
Peaking out at me

It bobs up and down
Waddling around all day long
Not a care in the world
A lovely little fellow

Its cute, little stare
Its enormous beak
Nothing will get in its way

A zany little guy
Standing, staring
Where did he go?
I think he went back to the woods
Waddling free

How I wish I was a kiwi!

Robert Paton (10)
Bridge of Weir Primary School

THE CAT

The cat
The ginger cat
The fierce, ginger cat
The fierce, ginger cat hunted
The fierce, ginger cat viciously hunted
The fierce, ginger cat viciously hunted the bird
The fierce, ginger cat viciously hunted the small bird
The fierce, ginger cat viciously hunted the small, frightened bird.

Craig Chamberlain (10)
Bridge of Weir Primary School

TIGER

I was walking in the jungle on a safari trip
When I saw a tiger prowling away
I followed him.

He leapt at a rabbit
He leapt at a hare
He crept up at a fox
He turned around
He looked at me
I thought he looked quite cute.

I heard something
He did too
He turned quickly
And jumped away.

Sarah Thomson (10)
Bridge of Weir Primary School

THE ZOMBIE

The zombie
The mean zombie
The mean, green zombie
The mean, green zombie burst
The mean, green zombie angrily burst
The mean, green zombie angrily burst through my bedroom door
The mean, green zombie angrily burst through my narrow
bedroom door
The mean, green zombie angrily burst through my narrow,
wooden bedroom door.

Christopher Mackie (10)
Bridge of Weir Primary School

THE FOOTBALLER

The footballer
The best footballer
The best Celtic footballer
The best Celtic footballer scored
The best Celtic footballer scored brilliantly
The best Celtic footballer scored brilliantly in front of the crowd
The best Celtic footballer scored brilliantly in front of the noisy crowd
The best Celtic footballer scored brilliantly in front of the noisy,
Cheering crowd.

Tom Kelly (10)
Bridge of Weir Primary School

THE DOLPHIN

The dolphin
The smooth dolphin
The smooth, blue dolphin
The smooth, blue dolphin played
The smooth, blue dolphin happily played
The smooth, blue dolphin happily played in the sea
The smooth, blue dolphin happily played in the big sea
The smooth, blue dolphin happily played in the big, wide sea.

Amanda Maxwell (10)
Bridge of Weir Primary School

LION

I saw a lion creeping up on its prey,
He pounced up, it never saw another day.
Feasting on its kill,
Lazing at the foot of his hill.

Agilely moving through the grass,
It's lunch time at last.
Alas, his day draws to an end,
Oh, how I wish to have the life of that lazy critter.

Matthew Bristow (10)
Bridge of Weir Primary School

THE WORLD

The world
The spheric world
The spheric, coloured world
The spheric, coloured world orbited
The spheric, coloured world slowly orbited
The spheric, coloured world slowly orbited round the sun
The spheric, coloured world slowly orbited round the red-hot sun
The spheric, coloured world slowly orbited round the flaming,
red-hot sun.

Michael Hardie (10)
Bridge of Weir Primary School

THE DOLPHIN

The dolphin
The friendly dolphin
The friendly, blue dolphin
The friendly, blue dolphin jumped
The friendly, blue dolphin happily jumped
The friendly, blue dolphin happily jumped into the water
The friendly, blue dolphin happily jumped into the deep water
The friendly, blue dolphin happily jumped into the deep, clear water.

Vhari Toole (10)
Bridge of Weir Primary School

THE TIGER

The tiger
The tired tiger
The tired, drowsy tiger
The tired, drowsy tiger yawned
The tired, drowsy tiger lazily yawned
The tired, drowsy tiger lazily yawned in the jungle
The tired, drowsy tiger lazily yawned in the dense jungle
The tired, drowsy tiger lazily yawned in the green, dense jungle.

Sandie Macdonald (10)
Bridge of Weir Primary School

THE FROG

The frog
The green frog
The green, croaking frog
The green, croaking frog hopped
The green, croaking frog happily hopped
The green, croaking frog happily hopped into the pond
The green, croaking frog happily hopped into the garden pond
The green, croaking frog happily hopped into the tiny garden pond.

Rebecca Cunningham (10)
Bridge of Weir Primary School

EAGLE

A big, sleek animal
Spying quietly for food
Get ready to pounce
Bend feet and *snatch!*

Tiptoe back with dinner in its mouth
On top of a tree, leap and swoosh
Fast, strong and brave is the eagle
Oh, why can't I fly high?

Louise Andrew (10)
Bridge of Weir Primary School

THE DOG

The dog
The cuddly dog
The cuddly, black dog
The cuddly, black dog jumped
The cuddly, black dog jumped high
The cuddly, black dog jumped high through the hoop
The cuddly, black dog jumped high through the large hoop
The cuddly, black dog jumped high through the large, round hoop.

Fiona Meldrum (10)
Bridge of Weir Primary School

THE KITTEN

The kitten
The shy kitten
The shy, white kitten
The shy, white kitten hid
The shy, white kitten slowly hid
The shy, white kitten slowly hid the ball
The shy, white kitten slowly hid the colourful ball
The shy, white kitten slowly hid the colourful, round ball.

Kerri Hunter (10)
Bridge of Weir Primary School

THE HAMSTER

The hamster
The vicious hamster
The vicious, white hamster
The vicious, white hamster bit
The vicious, white hamster painfully bit
The vicious, white hamster painfully bit my finger
The vicious, white hamster painfully bit my muddy finger
The vicious, white hamster painfully bit my muddy, tasty finger.

Lynne Mckenzie (9)
Bridge of Weir Primary School

THE GHOST

The ghost
The scary ghost
The scary, white ghost
The scary, white ghost moved
The scary, white ghost quickly moved
The scary, white ghost quickly moved through the wall
The scary, white ghost quickly moved through the thick wall
The scary, white ghost quickly moved through the thick, old wall.

Scott Mckenzie (10)
Bridge of Weir Primary School

LION

I saw a great big lion
Creeping ready to kill
Jerks all over the place
Grabbing a zebra down.

Chasing a little, brown bunny
Then runs home for dinner
Eats it all up
Now he's the winner.

Hannah Wright (10)
Bridge of Weir Primary School

THE SHARK

The shark
The fierce shark
The fierce, man-eating shark
The fierce, man-eating shark killed
The fierce, man-eating shark slowly killed
The fierce, man-eating shark slowly killed the squid
The fierce, man-eating shark slowly killed the large squid
The fierce, man-eating shark slowly killed the large, soft squid.

Christopher Murphy (10)
Bridge of Weir Primary School

THE GUINEA PIG

The guinea pig
The cute guinea pig
The cute, brown guinea pig
The cute, brown guinea pig played
The cute, brown guinea pig joyfully played
The cute, brown guinea pig joyfully played with its apple
The cute, brown guinea pig joyfully played with its huge apple
The cute, brown guinea pig joyfully played with its huge, juicy apple.

Laura Barney (10)
Bridge of Weir Primary School

Fox

The fox crept slowly through the bushes
And dodged the broken twigs
He sneaked past all the staring hens
He hid
He crouched
He pounced
And he got the hen.

I love the way he is so sly
I wonder if that will ever be me?

Rachael Ferguson (10)
Bridge of Weir Primary School

Owl

I see a silent hunter
About to pounce on prey
Flapping these massive wings
Soaring towards the ground
Miss, flying upwards
In a furious mood.

Feathers fly, she aims at me.

Carol Hunter (9)
Bridge of Weir Primary School

The Polar Bear

The little fluffy polar bear
Plodding clumsily through the Arctic
Sliding down the snowy hills
Oh, what a joy it would be
Standing in the cold, crisp air.

I have always wanted to be
Such a kind and sensitive animal
And who knows
One day I may be
Would you like to be?

Paul Stewart (10)
Bridge of Weir Primary School

TIGER

I saw a big, fierce tiger
He was creeping about the jungle
He pounced on a deer
And it was a rare one.

He had it for his dinner
And it was a winner.

I think I want to be a tiger.

Connor Stevenson (10)
Bridge of Weir Primary School

GUINEA PIG

I saw a baby guinea pig
Scamper in her run
Squeaking all the time
Gobbling every little bit of nutrients
She sleeps all night
And plays with me all day
Then we both get very tired
So off we go to bed.

Caroline Finlay (10)
Bridge of Weir Primary School

ELEPHANT

The elephant crashes through the jungle
Munching or bashing down trees
All animals fear it
It continues to go crashing through the jungle
Through villages
Through rivers
And over poachers
The elephant continues to run away from poachers
But there are too many of them
The elephant charges
The poachers run back to the village.

Michael Bell (10)
Bridge of Weir Primary School

EAGLE

Once I saw an eagle climb up into the sky
It soared and swooped and dived
It rose and rose above the clouds.

Its sleek, brown feathers
Its razor-sharp claws
Oh, how I wish I was that eagle
Soaring higher and higher.

Then it swooped down from the clouds
And snatched my hat away.

Adam Rushton (10)
Bridge of Weir Primary School

THE FALCON

I saw a small falcon flapping through a valley
In and out of the clouds he swiftly flew
And swerving in the air, faster than a jet
A tiny vole was caught in his sharp talons
About to slaughter the vole but it dropped.

He saw a pigeon
And he swooped down again
Got that pigeon!

And he was happy
Dancing in the air
Doing loop-the-loops.

I wish I was him
Not a care in the world.

Gary McCrossan (10)
Bridge of Weir Primary School

CHEETAH

I saw a young cheetah run
Through the long grass
And jump up a tree
A big and spotty cat
Stayed looking for its prey.

It turned and jumped away
He put his legs up to jump
It ran and caught a deer
Which was very rare.

Colin Guthrie (10)
Bridge of Weir Primary School

PEOPLE AND JOBS

Once there was a milkman called Fran,
He tried to flush his cat down the toilet pan,
It scratched him in the face,
And smashed his noggin' with a briefcase,
And he was never seen again.

Then there was a footballer,
Who was an awful bawler,
He woke up the street,
And the neighbours stamped on his feet,
And he was never seen again.

Once there was a tennis player called Pete,
Whose serve was really neat,
The ball smashed his opponent in the face,
And the umpire shouted, 'Ace!'
And he was never seen again.

Then there was a colonel called Blink,
He fell down his bathroom sink,
He was stuck there all night,
And he never again saw light,
And he was never seen again.

All the people who feature here,
Drank lots and lots of beer,
One day they all went insane,
And they were never seen again,
    Five steps to insanity.

Ryan Muldoon (11)
Craigielea Primary School

STARS

Stars twinkle up very high
To light up the dark blue sky
They shimmer and shine
Most of the time
They sparkle so bright and dance so high
And that's what brought a tear to my eye.

Then one night when the sky was clear
I saw a pretty star appear
But in the morning
When the stars have a rest
In the sky is a shining guest
The sun takes over in the day
At night the stars come out to play.

It must be hard to be a star
Cos you have to twinkle near and far
I suppose stars are just like candles
Even though they don't have handles
But someday I'll figure out
What stars are all about!

Kerry Ritchie (11)
Craigielea Primary School

THE BOY WHO HURT HIS KNEE

There was a small boy from Craigielea
Who fell and hurt his knee
He went to the nurse
She gave him her purse
And said, 'Go and get my tea.'

Robert Hamilton (11)
Craigielea Primary School

SCHOOL IS SO COOL

I like school
School is so cool
My friends and I rule
Sometimes I act like a fool.

School, school, school
School is so cool.

Some people hate school
But I think it is so cool
We run about mad
And think we are fab.

School, school, school
School is so cool.

We do our times tables
And alphabet too
We jump out at each other
And shout, *'Boo!'*

Lisa Thomas (11)
Craigielea Primary School

MY PET SNAKE

If I had a pet it would be a snake
I would call it Jake the snake
I would keep it in a glass tank under the stairs
Every day I would feed it rats
It would soon be nice and big.

It would be my secret
My mum wouldn't understand
She's terrified of snakes
If she found it she would scream
And hit it with a hammer.

So now I can only dream
Of what life would be like
With my pet snake, Jake,
But maybe when I'm older
My dream may come true.

Craig Whitelaw (11)
Craigielea Primary School

SHOOTING STARS

Once
I saw
a shooting star
it danced
across the sky.
It had a tail so
bright and
fell clear like
a teardrop
from my eye. Specks
of dust fell from its
gaze, it had sparkling
rays. The sky so dark,
the star so near. It
sparkled in the sky, it
twinkled in my eye. It shot
through space to Venus then
sparkled its way to Mars.
Then all of a sudden it
stopped. It twinkled then it
dropped. It landed in the
ocean. But it's sparkle
never stopped.

Tracey Hammond (11)
Craigielea Primary School

MY KITTEN

My kitten has blue eyes and they look at the sky
It has short whiskers and they twitch and twirl
She lies on my bed, as round as a curl.

It has the sweetest little eyes and ears
Which draws tears to my eyes
It has a soft, little voice
But I have no choice to answer and adore.

It hunts alone for its ice cream cone
When I'm sad and down
She's always around
On my bed or under the stairs.

It is white and black with spots on its back
One side is white, the other has spots
But she's my kitten.

Anne McCabe (11)
Craigielea Primary School

MILLER'S END

When we moved to Miller's End
Every afternoon at four
A thin shadow of shade
Quavered through the garden door.

Dressed in black from head to toe
With a veil about her head
To us it seemed as though
She came walking from the dead.

Leon Morrow (11)
Craigielea Primary School

SPACE SHUTTLE

S pace is a non-gravity place
P eople float straight away
A steroids are everywhere
C omets are shooting everywhere
E verywhere planets and moons.

S ky labs and space shuttles fly about
H eat from the sun makes you sweat
U ranus is blue
T he world is so small from space
T he galaxy is so big
L ittle moons, big planets
E verything in space is so cool.

Jamie Evans (11)
Craigielea Primary School

MY DAD

My dad's like a motor
He always breaks down
My dad's like an elf
He's got a big nose
My dad's like a fish
He's very fishy
My dad is a monkey
He's very, very hairy
My dad is like a dictionary
He's a thick wee book
My dad is like an elephant
You can't see through him.

Jordan Bruce (11)
Craigielea Primary School

POLLUTION

P ollution, pollution over it goes
O ver our houses
L eft, right, all round
L ike insects all about
U nder, over it goes
T owns are polluted with rubbish
I n our houses, in our clothes
O nto land
N ever let it harm you.

Darren McGregor (9)
Ferguslie Primary School

AUTUMN

A utumn is when leaves fall off the trees
U nder the trees there are leaves all different colours
T he wind is so draughty (and blows the leaves off the trees)
U nder the trees there we kick the leaves
M any people wear warm clothes because it is very cold
N ear the river there are leaves all around the water.

Nicole Cameron (9)
Ferguslie Primary School

AN ACROSTIC WITCH POEM

W itches are scary, scary, they come out at Hallowe'en
I cy cold winds to make us stay in the house
T is for trick or treating
C is for candy and creeping
H is for Hallowe'en when black cats come out.

Amanda Walls (9)
Ferguslie Primary School

SUNKEN TREASURE

On a hot summer's day
Swimming in a big deep pool
I saw a sparkle
I dived down
Got it!

I swam to the surface
I jumped out, shouting for my mum
'Look what I've found!
Gold coin, my treasure

Look, it's a Greek coin.'
I've kept it for a souvenir
And showed it to my friends.

Robert Hulley (11)
Gallowhill Primary School

THE HIDDEN TREASURE

Under the ground
Next to the beach,
I found a box, old and rusty,
Opening it, I found money,
Looking around, no one to be seen.
Picked up the money and ran.
At my house, I hid the treasure.

Later a man was on my bed,
Asking for the treasure
Then I woke up.
I gasped,
It was a nightmare!

Christopher Hamilton (11)
Gallowhill Primary School

SUNNY SUNDAY

I went to the beach with a friend
We went digging near the middle
we found a chest.
It was filled with gold, covered
in seaweed.
There were jewels, silver, gold
and bronze.
We thought it could belong to pirates,
so we took it back home and thought it out,
We took it back to the beach and
looked at it again.
That night we knew it belonged to pirates
and we took it to the museum.

Heather Corbett (10)
Gallowhill Primary School

HIDDEN SPADE

I looked in the garden,
Where is it?
Over there?
Nowhere!
So I went in to the shed
There it was!
I picked it up
Went outside
To dig.

Graeme MacPherson (10)
Gallowhill Primary School

UNDER THE DEEP SEA

H idden in the deep
I n the oceans
D own in the dumps
D ark, creepy and scary
E ngines blowing
N oises made.

T reasures found and
R eceived.
E verything sparkling
A nd chests found
S cuba-divers diving
U nder the deep blue sea
R ivers flowing
E ngines blowing
S ome people are rich.

John Currie (11)
Gallowhill Primary School

RUNAWAY RING

I've lost my ring
Where could it be?
It's red and gold
And belongs to me
It's big and round
And should be found
And let's just hope
It's safe and sound.

Stewart White (10)
Gallowhill Primary School

GOLD LOCKET

I was in my gran's kitchen
A long, long time ago,
When suddenly I saw a bird fly
Through the window.

It had a message on its foot
I stood there and had a look
Then it fell on to the floor
And a knock came from the door.

I ran to the door to see who was there,
No one but a teddy bear
It also had a note
It said . . . 'Coat'.

I ran to the kitchen to get the bird's note
It also said 'Coat'.
I ran to my coat pocket and found a gold locket,
I went and showed my gran and she said to me . . .

'My mum gave this to me,
To show how happy she was to have me, her daughter Lee,
And now I give this to you to show I'm happy too!'

Nicola Archibald (11)
Gallowhill Primary School

A LUCKY DAY

Pirates, pirates everywhere
Getting chased by a grizzly bear.
Looking for hidden treasure
Is it here or there?
The other one asked
'Is it anywhere?'

Then, hey, it's my lucky day!
From now on I won't have to pay
Everybody in this town
Will know me from far around
Now I've found my hidden treasure.

Leigh-Anne Reddick (9)
Gallowhill Primary School

A WONDERFUL FIND

I was walking along the beach one day
when I came to a dingy.
I shouted 'Is anyone there?'
No reply
so I jumped into the dingy
and rowed it out to sea.

I rowed and rowed until my arms
started to hurt.
I stopped for a rest, but the dingy
drifted out.
I found myself beside a ship,
a big, ugly, brown ship.

I hopped on board and started to explore,
I fell through the floor into a
dark room.
I found an old, old box, but it was locked.

I found a hammer and broke the lock,
I opened the box and what did I find,
but a box full of gold before me.
It really was a wonderful find.

Raymond Paul (11)
Gallowhill Primary School

MY DOG'S TREASURE

It could be a ball or a bone
A twig or a chew,
If you try and take it she'll try and bite you.
My dog loves to treasure what she likes so much.

She has treasure in the garden, treasure in the house,
Nobody knows where it's hidden, because she is so sneaky.
Even if the treasure is big.

My dog dreams of balls,
Her legs twitch all night,
Thinking about playing in the park with me,
She loves her dinner, she eats it so fast,
Even if she's had a big lunch.

She gets a bit tired, so she goes for a sleep,
She went under the covers, and what did she see?
A big, giant bone, covered in gold.

Mark McNicholl (11)
Gallowhill Primary School

TREASURE

Treasure can be anything
Gold, silver or bronze
It could be
Underneath the deep sea
Or in your garden pond.

Treasure can be wet or dry,
Or buried and covered with mud.
Treasure can be on your plate
Covered up with spuds.

People have different things
Valuable or cheap.
But it doesn't matter what you have
It's always yours to keep.

Laura Benson   (11)
Gallowhill Primary School

THE £20 NOTE

When I was on a fancy boat,
I found a strange £20 note.
It didn't look like it was from here,
It could have been from far or near.
I checked if anyone was around
Then I heard the strangest sound.

I looked up and there it was
A bird with enormous jaws,
I put the boat's engine on
I then looked up! The thing was gone.

When I got to the pier,
That noise again, I could hear!
But the thing did not appear,
I started to get scared.

It must have been that £20 note,
Which I found on the boat.
I ran over to the bin
And threw the £20 note in.

Suddenly I woke up
Lying in my bed,
Then I knew that it
Was all in my head.

Seumais Peter Simpson (11)
Gallowhill Primary School

OCEAN BLUE

Far away deep
Right under in the ocean blue
There is treasure, just for me
Not you.
No one will come, no one will see
Just me and not you.
In the deep blue sea.

Far away deep
Right under in the ocean blue
The treasure still lies beneath
I can't wait until I can go.
Having parties with all my treasure/
Just me and not you!

But then my mum came in
And woke me up.
Now I only dream.
Some day . . .
Just for me, not you
In the ocean blue.

Nicole Andrews (10)
Gallowhill Primary School

TREASURE'S BEEN STOLEN

Diamonds, goblets, gems galore,
Found in a chest beyond the shore,
Pirates hide the chest away
Their island, they are there to stay.

Travelling far, upon their boat
The captain puts diamonds on his coat.
I wish I could get that treasure,
I will sell them coats of leather.

I have found the coats of leather
Now I can trick them, for the treasure.
My plan has failed, it's time to cry
The leather coats they did not buy.

The climate here is very low,
We have lots of ice and snow.
I will jump into the sea
So they will come and capture me.

Stephanie Stewart (10)
Gallowhill Primary School

Wonderful, Amazing, Fantastic

Moving house
One day moved in
A young girl
up in the attic
found a shining chest.

Moving house
Wonderful, amazing, fantastic
Gold,
Jewels,
Silver.
Wow!

Up in the attic
dusty
old
crooked.
But no! This
shining treasure
just made my day.

Linzi Hanratty (11)
Gallowhill Primary School

Rusty Chest

Deep down under the sea
Where all the fish live
The archaeologists were looking for clues
To find hidden treasure.

With gold in it,
Bronze, jewels, silver
And even diamonds,
Then they come over a rusty chest.

Then they came over the sand they opened it,
They had found what they were looking for
And there was a map with a red 'X' on it,
Hooray!

Stephanie Cooney (10)
Gallowhill Primary School

Money!

Finding hidden treasure, is a pirate's aim.
Long John Silver found it along with some great fame.
Find the map and there you go,
You've got a great big clue.
To find the chest all filled with gold, coins of
Silver too
We've found the hidden treasure, it's where X
Marks the spot.
We'll take it home and count it and
Spend the entire lot!

Kerrys Stevenson (10)
Gallowhill Primary School

FAR, FAR DOWN TO SEA

I remember when I was little,
I went far, far down to sea.

To my surprise, I happened to find
An old treasure chest you see!

With sharks and piranha fish,
I was still so very brave,
That I happened to go down and open it,
That was a very close shave.

It had jewels and diamonds and emeralds in
And a big cup made of gold.

So I gathered it up and rushed back
Up to the surface, before I got cold.

Danielle McMeekin (11)
Gallowhill Primary School

CHOCOLATE PENNIES

I found some buried treasures
Down in the deep blue sea.
You see it was not ordinary treasures
It was chocolate treasure,
You know, chocolate treasure
It's normally gold or silver
You sometimes find a necklace or two
But all I found was chocolate pennies.

Stacey Moyes (11)
Gallowhill Primary School

HIDDEN TREASURES

H   idden treasures
I   n the sea
D   eep, deep down
D   own and down
E   very different kind of creature
N   o one dips, but they all dive into the water.

T   o find the treasures
R   ound the seas
E   very day
A   way and away
S   wimmers and swimmers
U   nder the sea
R   ough and tough
E   very day
S   o the treasure is found!

Danielle Gallacher (11)
Gallowhill Primary School

GOLD

As I go diving under the sea,
I discover some bones and a chest.
I try to get the chest open
When an octopus appears.
I swim to the shore and go and get
Archaeologists and scuba-divers
To try and get the chest open.
I get the chest open and I discover
Gold, bronze and silver.

Simone Footitt (10)
Gallowhill Primary School

A Hundred Million Quid

A hundred million quid
Now that's a lot of money!
If I had that amount of cash
I'd give some to my mummy.
I'd give some to my dad
And my little sister too.
Then the first thing I would buy
Is a PlayStation 2.
I'd give my grans some gold,
And get my paps a car.
I'd give my aunt and uncle cash
So they could travel far.
Then I'd put some in the bank,
To let it grow and grow.
So when I get much older,
A fortune I would show.

Kieron McLardie (10)
Gallowhill Primary School

The City Of Chuba Chub Land

One day I met some archaeologists
They told me I had to go deep under the sea
So they took me to my submarine.
It looked like a lemonade bottle,
Two hours later, I was nearly there
Then some piranha fish gathered around the bottle
Luckily, the cork was in.
To my relief, I had finally reached the city.

Ryan Love (10)
Gallowhill Primary School

OVER THE WAVES

They sailed for thirty nights and days
Through the storms and over the waves
To get the treasure, which lies far away.

Land could be seen
And the sailors rejoiced!
The captain sailed on
With all his might.

Then they arrived at the sandy island
And started looking immediately.
They didn't stop to eat or sleep
They didn't stop for a few weeks.

But then they hit something hard,
They dug a mole, then heaved it out
'Twas treasure and it made them
Cheer and shout,
As they were going to open it
A sailor with a few men, stole the treasure.
It was so sudden
That no one caught them!

On the ship the sailor opened the chest,
But inside the chest there was nothing.
But the sailor only grinned and said . . .
'Perfect!'

Kim Black (9)
Gallowhill Primary School

LOST AND FOUND

I moved into my new house
I looked all around.
I visited the basement but only
Found a pound,
I looked all around
I found this little box
Inside the box was
Gold, silver, pearls and money,
Jewels and rings.
I thought these weren't real
I picked one up and didn't want to steal
I shouted to my mum
To come downstairs
I told her what it was
She nearly fell down the stairs.
She came running over to the box
She said 'You'll have to take it to the police.'
I took it to the police.
The man asked me where I'd found it,
I had to give the policeman a statement,
Six months later, the police phoned me
They said that nobody had come to claim it,
So I could come and collect it.
I got the gold.
I gave it to my gran, mum, dad and papa.
My gran was so happy.
She battered my papa.

Gary Dean (11)
Gallowhill Primary School

THE TREASURE IN THE GARDEN

I was digging in the garden
Until I found . . .
A big sparkling diamond
Shining, round and round.
I picked it up and said
'Hello,
You've lost your owner, you poor wee soul.
I'll try and find who you belong to.
Then you'll be safe and sound.
But if I cannot find your owner
It means you're lost.
I'll try and try, until luck comes my way.
We'll say goodbye, because we're on our way
But if I cannot find them, you'll be my hidden treasure.
You'll become my hidden treasure of the year
I'll hand you into the police
I'll say I found you in the garden.'
So I did that and they said 'Thank you!'
And six months later I got a letter through the post
With a sharp thing in it.
I opened it up and there it was
My hidden treasure!

Lauren Swanson (11)
Gallowhill Primary School

THE HIDDEN TREASURE

When I was a boy
I went on holiday,
Staying near the beach.
One night, thunder and lightning struck.
It struck so bad, the lights went out
It was raining so heavy
The rain ran from the gutters

The next morning,
The beach was split in half,
Jumped into the hole
Saw a box
Old, dirty and rusty
When I got home
I opened it and
It's full of gold and silver.

Thomas Wright (11)
Gallowhill Primary School

TREASURE, TREASURE

Treasure, treasure, where can you be?
Treasure, treasure, maybe under the sea?
Way under the deep, dark waves
For many, many, deep dark days.

Go under the sea with a big submarine,
Red, blue or maybe green.
Whales, jellyfish and fish
Some people think they are nice on a dish.

I spot a sunken ship
Then I bite my bottom lip.
Maybe there is treasure,
Or maybe there is a shark.

I go in with my green submarine,
There is a bright shining light.
I ask myself what can it be?
Then I realised I had found the treasure.

Christina Rankin (11)
Gallowhill Primary School

THE MISSING NECKLACE

Treasure, rubies, gold and silver
You would say that's all a pirate wants,
But you were wrong, there is a pirate called
Silver Tooth.
And all that Silver Tooth wanted was her
Gold love heart chain.
She pulled out everything, just trying to find
Her gold love-heart chain,
She tries to remember where she put it,
Just then, she remembers, it's in her treasure box.
She is relieved to have finally found her
Gold heart chain.

Clair Lochrie (10)
Gallowhill Primary School

THE IRISH SEA

T   he divers looking for treasure deep down in the Irish Sea
R   ushing down to the bottom of the Irish Sea
E   very day, the boat goes into the Irish Sea
A   t last they find the chest, deep down in the Irish Sea
S   oon they will bring it from the bottom of the Irish Sea
U   nder the chest there was a note, there's more treasure in the Irish Sea
R   eady the next morning to find more treasure in the Irish Sea
E   very one tried to find more treasure, but nobody ever found it in the
    Irish Sea.

Scott McPherson (9)
Gallowhill Primary School

OUR TEACHER

Miss Harper is our teacher,
She's like candyfloss,
She's a Barbie doll feature!
And she's got perfect hair to toss.

The colour of her hair,
Went from purple to blue to pink,
We all really care,
If she ever stops to think.

Davie is her boyfriend,
He's so very smart,
He's always got a hand to lend,
Unless of course it's art.

Her favourite thing is glitter,
Her favourite drink is coffee,
She'd become a lot fitter,
If her chocolate was fat-free.

She's taught us two times two,
And much more than any other,
High heels are her favourite shoe,
And she's got a cool wee brother.

Now we've heard about Miss Harper,
Who teaches P7/6,
I thought you'd be more sharper,
And discover who is next.

Ruaridh Hamilton (11)
Highholm Primary School

MY DAD

My dad is very special to me,
At home, he fills me up with glee.
But at night it's not quite the same,
When I'm snuggled in my bed, he makes me feel quite tame!

He really is a super dad
But at times he goes really mad!
His hobby is to go to the gym,
And that's what makes him feel quite slim.

At times he acts really weird,
And believe it or not he's thinking of growing a beard!
When it turns to the holidays, he does not shave,
And that's when my mum tells him to behave!

When it's night and it turns dark
I think he's going really berserk!
Then it starts to get really boring,
When I have to listen to him snoring.

So that is my dad for you,
If you want to see him, you'll have to join the queue.
That's because he's very special to me,
Oooh and the rest of the famileee!

Laura Hamilton (10)
Highholm Primary School

JESSIE

My puppy Jessie is very clever,
She likes to sleep forever and ever.
My puppy Jessie is very fluffy,
But sometimes she is very huffy!

My puppy Jessie is such a pain,
Sometimes I tell her to go away!
My puppy Jessie runs away,
But sometimes she just likes to play!

My puppy Jessie is so sweet,
Sometimes I like to give her a treat.
My puppy Jessie is so loveable,
Sometimes I just want to cuddle her.

My puppy Jessie is a star!

Elizabeth McKay (10)
Highholm Primary School

MY CAT CHUCKY

My cat's name is Chucky,
His paws are always mucky,
When he scratches the chair,
My mum goes absolutely spare.

His colour is black and white,
Black, as black as night,
When he sits on your knee,
He purrs just like a bee.

Some people think he's cute,
Until he scratches your foot,
He is very loveable,
But sometimes lots of trouble.

When you start to write,
Your pencil, he tries to bite,
And when I'm sleeping in bed,
He comes and sits upon my head.

So now you think you know my cat,
But you're wrong, there's more than that,
A cat is such a loyal friend,
They'll be with you to the bitter end.

Gareth Lindsay (11)
Highholm Primary School

My Sisters

I have two sisters
One is called Shona
She is like an angel
She never is a moaner.

I feel trouble
Here Morvern comes
Stop playing the heavenly harps
And beat the devil drums.

But that was Morvern in the past
She is now very good
But if you get on her nerves
She'll get in such a mood.

But back to Shona, she has blonde hair
Her age is twenty-three
She lives with her boyfriend in a flat
And she's very kind to me.

I love them both and they love me
I'm lucky to have them as sisters
Once when we went Christmas shopping
Morvern got two big blisters!

Jamie McLeod (10)
Highholm Primary School

My Dog Zorro

My dog Zorro is black and brown,
And sometimes he is such a clown,
He slips off my bed in the middle of the night,
And gives himself such a fright.

When I take him a walk he runs ahead,
And doesn't come back till he wants fed,
The only time he takes a seat,
Is when I give him a treat!

He is now five and a half and very black,
And loves to sleep in the dark,
At the top of the stairs he will go to sleep,
And Dad trips over him with big fat feet.

But he is my dog because he is mine,
And as a mongrel he is really fine,
So let us go Zorro,
And take a walk.

Graeme Hendry (11)
Highholm Primary School

MY MUM

My mum makes me happy
When I am feeling down,
My mum makes me sad
When she gives me a row.

My mum is quite small
Compared to the rest
Of the family
They are quite tall.

My mum is quite crazy
But sometimes she is lazy
When she sits on her bum
Watching the TV.

My mum has green eyes
Her age is thirty-six
Her favourite hobby is reading
She used to like to knit.

Even though my mum is crazy and lazy
She is like no other mum
She is the best in the world.

Emma Stoddart (11)
Highholm Primary School

MY BROTHER

My brother's name is Martin
He cuddles me all the time
He's seventeen years old
He annoys me from time to time.

When we scream
And shout
We have to fall out.

My brother is tall, he's like a big elephant.
He's 6ft 2"
He's not like you.

My brother has a hobby,
He likes to golf with my dad
When he's not, he's really sad.

My mum gets him into trouble
When he's really bad.

So that's my brother Martin
I hope you like him too.

Ailsa Craynor (11)
Highholm Primary School

MY DAD

My dad makes me happy and sad,
Sometimes he gets very mad.
My dad drinks a lot of beer,
A bit too much at New Year!

My dad is sometimes really crazy,
But mostly he is pretty lazy!
My dad sits at the computer all day,
So mostly I just go out and play.

My dad has got short, black hair,
Though there are grey bits everywhere.
I don't care if my dad is mad -
He's the best dad I've ever had!

Siobhan Hendry (11)
Highholm Primary School

MY BUDGIE BUTCH

My budgie Butch sits in his cage,
He flaps his wings and sings in rage.
He likes to peck and nibble seeds,
And I like to care for all his needs.

Butch is small and very fluffy,
Without his mirror, he gets quite huffy.
He's really green
And very mean.

He's really messy
But awfully dressy.
He's good at flapping
But better at napping!

He's a very small height
But really bright
He's got a big beak
And gives lots of cheek!

My budgie Butch sits in his cage,
He flaps his wings and sings in rage.
He likes to peck and nibble seeds,
And I like to care for all his needs.

Matthew Carnegie (11)
Highholm Primary School

MY BROTHER

I love my brother!
He adores me and my mother.
He is so loveable,
But for my mum that's twice the trouble!

He's got strawberry-blond hair and bright blue eyes,
And never cries but always lies.
He is very giggly and funny,
He likes playing shops because of the money!

That's my brother,
He's something else.
He's a pain in the neck,
But he's the best!

He loves to play with his teddy bear,
And that makes my mum go spare.
He always wants me to play,
But I don't have the time of day!

Carrie Gallacher (10)
Highholm Primary School

MY DAD AND HIS BED

My dad loves to sleep,
On the bed or the couch,
Counting white, fluffy sheep,
He lets out a big slouch.

My dad's hobby is snoring,
It makes a droning sound,
It is very boring,
But he eventually comes round.

He likes to go for forty winks,
And dreams of golf in the sun.
When he sleeps, all he thinks is . . .
Can I get a hole in one?

My dad is a peaceful man . . .
When he falls asleep.
I am his greatest fan,
When he's counting hundreds of sheep!

Ryan Kane (10)
Highholm Primary School

MY BROTHER GREG

I have a brother whose name is Greg
He likes to joke and pull my leg!
When he's feeling down -
He makes a frown
Even at me, if I didn't make a sound!

He's got black hair and sits in a chair
And plays his guitar all day.

He's 15 years old
And I don't know the things he's told.
He's always in my way -
But goes to the golf course every day.
He does 18 holes
With only three poles.
When he stands near, I feel quite wee.
As much as he can make me mad -
If he wasn't here, it would make me sad.

Craig Hill (10)
Highholm Primary School

THE WATERFRONT

I love going to the pool
The thing I hate the most is all the rules.
I like to go through the waves
But I normally come up in a daze!

And also something about splashing
Makes it absolutely smashing.
I can stay underwater for 23 seconds
And that is more than what I reckoned.

The flumes are fast and slow
But I like the tyre flume, it's a nice slow flow.
The faster one you can see outside
But it's really scary from the inside!

The jacuzzi is very hot -
It can hold eight people at the lot.
There's a children's area right beside it . . .
And lots of children have fun inside it.

Ryan Cheshire (10)
Highholm Primary School

MY BROTHER

My brother Paul is very tall,
Sometimes he likes to play football,
Judo is his favourite hobby,
When he was younger he liked Mr Blobby.

My brother thinks he is very cool,
He really likes the swimming pool,
When he goes down the twisty flume,
He likes to shout, '*Zoom, zoom!*'

I think he is clever,
I will love him forever,
There is no other,
Than my little brother.

Martyn Wotherspoon (10)
Highholm Primary School

MY NEPHEW

My nephew Josh,
He's always asking for dosh,
But that's just Josh,
He's certainly not posh.

He loves his gun,
And he loves to run,
He is very fun,
In the sun.

Josh is three,
And he's really wee,
He's just like me,
When he eats his tea.

He is very small,
And he loves football,
He likes to go to the mall,
And terrify them all.

My nephew I like to care,
My wee Josh is always there,
I love the way he plays with my hair,
And rolls all around the 'fler'.

Kerry Thompson (11)
Highholm Primary School

TOM MY CAT!

Tom is my cat,
As black as a bat.
He loves big cuddles,
And on cold nights, loves to snuggle.

He's seven years old,
Still big and bold.
He likes a pat on the head,
And sleeps in my bed.

His whiskers are black,
He never attacks.
His eyes are green,
He's gone to places I've never been.

He follows me up the street,
Oh I think he deserves a treat.
I think he's the best,
Oh so better than all the rest.

Sara Knox (11)
Highholm Primary School

MY BROTHER

My brother makes me laugh!
He always laughs at me,
But that doesn't matter 'cause
He's part of the family.

Well, he is quite tall,
Has brown hair and long sidies.
He always wears a pair of raggy jeans
That look a mess.

Well he thinks he's cool,
But he isn't, just because he's a skater.
But you see his sidies they are as big as a tree,
And he's bigger than my dad.

Amy Laura Woodcock (11)
Highholm Primary School

MY DOG MEGAN

I have a dog
whose name is Megan
who thinks she's a pup
but doesn't have much luck

She can run very fast
but doesn't know the way
usually trying to catch her tail
in a very odd way

If she was human
she would need medical help
because her mental health
is in very much doubt

She sleeps in a king size bed
but acts like the Queen
expecting good service
her bowl's always clean

I love her to bits
even her mad ways
because she is mental Meg
the pup with no brains!

Jonathan Ferguson (11)
Highholm Primary School

MY DAD

My dad is fat,
Although he'd kill me if I told you that,
Just read this poem,
If you want to know him.

I love my dad because he's really funny,
Especially when he makes fun of Mummy,
My little sister gets all the attention,
Me? No! Not even a mention.

My dad has ginger sidies,
Which he never, ever tidies,
He thinks he's cool, he's 38,
But to me and my friends he's just out of date.

He's quite greedy when it comes to food,
And he is so very rude,
He has multicoloured hair,
Which will always be there.

My dad has got spiky cheeks,
Because he hasn't shaved for weeks,
He works in Holland which I think is cool,
I tell everyone, even in school.

He always takes control of the TV,
Just think yourself lucky you aren't me,
How does he watch it with his eyes closed tight,
And see me making faces when I'm out of sight?

So that's my dad packed all in one,
And I am his oldest son,
Just look at your dad and see if he's like mine,
You never know, there might be a sign.

Thomas Wilson (10)
Highholm Primary School

MY MEMORIES

Locked away safely
are my memories.

A holiday to Disneyland, Paris
where I met Mickey Mouse.
The birth of my cousin Robyn
when I got to choose her name.
My sixth birthday
when my bedroom was decorated in my best colours.
My uncle's wedding
when I was asked to be a flower girl.
At the millennium
when we had a celebration with all our neighbours.

Some day in the future
I'll share these precious times.

Jennifer Priestley (8)
Houston Primary School

MY WISHING POT

Inside my wishing pot
there are a thousand wishes.

I would like a sleepover so my friends can have some fun,
I'm going to do better writing so people can understand,
A baby brother or sister so I can help my mum,
Or maybe a horse or pony so I can take it places.

They are trying to get out!
But I run before they get away
And smack the lid shut.

Christina Bardell (8)
Houston Primary School

MEMORIES

I have memories of everything I've done
Some of laughter, some of fun.

Receiving a bunch of flowers
Lilies and roses.

Sliding down a mountain
Coming down at a very fast speed.

My first time at a party
Wearing a green frock and sandals.

Going to a beach
With the sand running through my toes.

The day I went to a dancing class
And learnt to do ballet.

Those are just a few of my memories
Because I have millions more.

Jessica Maskrey (8)
Houston Primary School

SNOWY

Snowflakes dropping, snowflakes falling.
The snow is covering everything in the town.
Snow is everywhere in the village.
People outside having lots of snowball fights,
Making snowmen, lots of children having lots of fun.
The snow is a big, white sheet just fallen from the sky.
Lots of children putting on scarves and putting on hats and gloves.
It's cold.

Ben Chapman (9)
Houston Primary School

MY COLOUR BOX

Looking inside my
pale blue colour box, I can see:

Orange as
burning as lava flowing down a volcano.
Silver as
hard as waves crashing on the shore.
Gold as
the sun in summer skies.
Black as
a deep, dark cave at night.
Red as
a shepherd's warning in the morning.

Now I must close the lid
before the colours escape.

Ellen Robinson (8)
Houston Primary School

STORM

Blowing hard against my window.
Wakes me up during the night,
Oh, I got a terrible fright,
Oh, what a horrible Monday.
Looking out
Oh my!
Just what a horrible Monday.
Dustbins here, there and everywhere.
Oh Scotland, oh Scotland for *weather*
But I am in the house all cosy and warm.

Emma Hollinsworth (9)
Houston Primary School

THE NIGHTMARE BOX

Last week, I had some nightmares
They were very creepy.

Zombies
A bony zombie I wouldn't go near.
Ghosts
Very spooky and creepy.
Buried alive
It is very dark down here.
Being lunch to aliens
Very, very gross.
Giant cobra
The venom kills me.

I tried to get them out of my head
But they would not go.

Grier McDonald Porch (8)
Houston Primary School

STORM

All I see
All I see
Is a naked large tree.
Tiles flying all around
Even some on the ground.

Dustbins fly away over there
Some could be anywhere.
The terrible weather whooshes all around
But I was in the house safe and sound!

Douglas Holmes (9)
Houston Primary School

MY COLOUR BOX

Looking inside my colour box,
The colours I can see -
Yellow,
Bright like sunshine.
A red,
So full of warmth.
Orange,
Looks just like fire.
Black,
So dark and cold.
And last, a blue,
Almost twins with the sky.
Now I'd better close the lid,
Before they all fade away.

Stuart Black (8)
Houston Primary School

TERROR WIND

Wind,
It blows down trees,
It terrorises houses,
And I wonder why it knocks over fences,
It can lift gates off their hinges,
It destroys anything it wants,
And no one can stop it.

And then it goes through the town,
Peaceful and gentle,
Then suddenly it jumps into action,
It starts blowing as hard as it can,
And then it begins all over again.

Blair Meikle (9)
Houston Primary School

MY JAR OF SOUNDS

In my jar of sounds
it's full to the brim.

Fire engine
   rushing to a fire.
Rain battering
   on the windowpane
Dog barking
   because it wants food.
People
   shouting for attention.
Hear my hamsters
   squeaking for food.

I'll close my lid with a snap
and bury it before it's sounds fly out.

Kirsty Horn (8)
Houston Primary School

STORMY

Blowing hard against my windows
Wake up startled!
Howling curtains moving
Looking out
Oh my!
Fences blown down
Tiles flying down!
Blowing a gale
I hate it!
Blowing people off their feet!
Knocking the lamp posts and cars over.

David Greig (9)
Houston Primary School

MY BOX OF MEMORIES

I have a box of memories
full to the brim.
My first day at school
in my school dress and buckle shoes.
My first bike
with stabilisers and a helmet.
At playgroup
playing with playdough.
Meeting Katy
at toddlers.
Seeing The Singing Kettle
with all my friends.
Make a moat around it
before they disintegrate.

Julie Richmond (8)
Houston Primary School

SNOW

Gentle snow falling to the ground
I wake up in the morning and hear the sound
Children's joyful cries all day long
The morning birds break into song
The boys on their sledges, look how they go
Down on the hill covered in snow.

I put on my hat and coat
And my big, black boots
And go out to play
On this beautiful snowy day.
I roll a ball so big and strong
I hear the church bells go ding, dang, dong.

Craig Howie (9)
Houston Primary School

MY WISHING BOX

Inside my wishing box
there are a million wishes.

To have a big brother or sister
and then I could play with them every day.
To meet Hear'say
because they are my favourite band.
To be happy
so everyone can live joyfully.
To get £1 every month
so I could be richer.

Surround it with a moat
and lock the magic inside.

Kirsty Murray (8)
Houston Primary School

STORM

Blowing, blowing, the wind is blowing.
Trucks tipping over on the roads.
Fences falling over.
Cars in car parks on their sides.
Bus shelters out of place.
Getting blown everywhere.
Wind, wind, everywhere.
Lamp posts down,
On the ground.
Trees with branches breaking out and flying everywhere.
Birds flying everywhere.
People coming off their feet.

Ryan McMaster (9)
Houston Primary School

A MESS I TELL YOU!

Blows down trees,
Fences, houses, lorries, cars,
We all get blown off our feet,
A mess I tell you!
Trees been blown on the road,
Lorries on the motorway,
Fences blown down at the back of houses.
Disaster everywhere.
Birds are flying everywhere.
Up and down,
Up and down,
Down, round and round,
A mess I tell you!
Ridge tiles fallen off roofs
As well as lamp posts leaning over.

Gemma Robertson (9)
Houston Primary School

THE BIG WINDY DAY

Wind, wind, coming to town.
Big winds, dangerous winds,
Blowing down fences, trees, aerials.
Trees and lorries overturned!
Wind shooting up my spine
Whistling round buildings, oh dear!
Blowing water over fences.
People blown off their feet.
People blown against buildings,
But I am safe inside my house.

Scott Whyte (9)
Houston Primary School

A STORMY DAY

Stormy wind, banging against my window,
I woke up with a fright.

Trees flying all around,
tiles and slates lying all around.
Fences, lorries and other things,
'I can't believe what mess it brings!'
The terrible wind blows everything around
but I was safe and sound.
People cheering as the wind goes away
I'll never forget that windy day.
Bins flying all around.
Children walking to school
almost breaking their bones from the stones.

Cara Drummond (9)
Houston Primary School

WILD WIND

Wind is coming on its way, up and down the alleyway
Swinging and blowing up and down, birds are flying round and round.
Roofs are flying everywhere, glass is blowing on the stair.
We are happy on the way, we are all blowing away.
Up and down the motorway, cars are bringing spiky sprays.
Round and round the river goes, in and out the river flows.
Aerials fall to the ground, over and over all day long.
It sprays up and down until eventually it comes back down.
Oh Scotland! Oh Scotland! Until the wind goes away, we will

all blow away.

Oh Scotland! Oh Scotland!

Emma Whyte (9)
Houston Primary School

MY POT OF COLOURS

I have a pot of many colours
here are some.
Red
    the colour of a bright red ball.
Yellow
    the colour of the sun.
Pink
    the colour of a big pink pig.
Blue
    the colour of the big blue sky.
Orange
    the colour of a big juicy orange.
Now I close it tightly
before they drain away.

Katy Richardson (8)
Houston Primary School

WINDY DAYS

Wind blowing against the fence.
Wind blowing against the trench.
Howling and screaming on the bench.
It is making such a mess.
Here and there.
It is blowing everywhere.
Blowing the seawrecking ships.
All they see is swirling swings.
Up and down, pushing people off their ground.
Trees are flying off the ground on their roots.

Lee Adam (9)
Houston Primary School

MY JAR OF SOUNDS

I have a box
with lots of sound
gentle whispering sounds
throughout the house.
A big steady beat coming
from the garage.
A chit-chat noise
in our big room.
Pit-pat, pit-pat
upon the roof.
Loud drum sounds
from down the street.
Hurry, close it quick
before they all escape.

Heather Kirkland (8)
Houston Primary School

STORM DAY

Howling wind blowing against my windows
I look out, a tree is falling,
Oh my!
Blowing down fences,
Shouting and bashing.

I go outside, the wind blows me over,
Branches litter the ground,
How can I stop it?
It batters off the house,
Throws dustbins here and there,
How can I stop it?

Alastair Griffiths (9)
Houston Primary School

STORM

The wind was blowing at my window
I woke with a fright!
The rain was banging on the roof.
My curtains were waving everywhere.
I looked out of my window, it was a mess.
I went to school, I nearly got blown off my feet.
A tree fell down with a crash.
Leaves were blowing in my face.
My hat was blowing off my head.
I wish I could have stayed in bed.
I got into school, I took off my coat.
Soaked right through.
A window nearly blew out of place.
Quite scary.
I thought the school would blow down.

Ryan Blair (9)
Houston Primary School

WIND, WIND, WIND

Wind, wind banging against my windowpane.
Howling like a hurricane.
I woke up in shock,
Wind, wind flying everywhere,
Shouting anywhere.
Lots of disasters.
Everywhere trees fall,
Rivers flood.
Oh it was the wind,
Wind, wind.

Rebecca McCluskie (9)
Houston Primary School

THE NIGHT WIND

Blowing, blowing against my window
I could hear it
Woke up startled!
Windows shook
Looked out
Oh my!
I shouted to my mum
And told her I was scared!
Tiles blowing around
And branches broken from trees
Windows flying open
The morning came and it still went on
I was off to school in a flurry.

Lindsay McLellan (9)
Houston Primary School

STORM

The heavy wind blowing against the window
Wake up scared!
Howling, covers moving
Look out
Oh my!
Tiles falling from the roofs
Trees fallen down
Fences blown over
Very scary.
I went to school
Had to hold my jacket tight
Walked to school with the wind roaring in my ears.

Cameron Sim (9)
Houston Primary School

THE STORM

When I wake up in the morning
I feel something; global warming.
I think what could it be?
I look out the window, what do I see . . .
Oh no!
Cars, lorries, fences, dustbins,
All blown over on the road.
People walking on the pavement shivering
With the wind blowing in their hair
And their dogs nearly blowing away.
Lots of people running for shelter
But I'm in here
Safe and sound.

Murray Noble (9)
Houston Primary School

A TERRIBLE STORM

The wind was blowing hard.
Roof tiles coming off.
Oh what a terrible Monday.
Bang! A fence had blown over.
Trees were falling down, crash!
Lorries overturned.
Oh what a terrible Monday.
I got a fright because I woke up in the night.
People scared out of their wits.
Even I was scared and I'm sure you were too.
Dustbins here, dustbins there,
Some could be anywhere.

Adam MacAlister (9)
Houston Primary School

WIND

Howling!
Blowing!
Against my window
That's what I heard,
The wind!
When I woke I looked out my window
Lots!
Lots!
Lots of slates off my roof
On the ground.
Walking to school
Oh dear!
Oh my!
The building silent
Door blown off the van
I walk on
I see lots of slates all over the ground
I get to school
I am playing, it's fun
Getting blown over by the wind
But getting warm is nice in the school.

Jack Doak (9)
Houston Primary School

WIND

The wind twists and whirls like a chocolate milkshake.
It whips across my face like a whip in the circus.
It can damage houses, fences and lorries.
It will die down some day but soon it will come back again.

Fiona Hunter (9)
Houston Primary School

THE WIND

Blowing against my window
Woke up and screamed out loud!
Roaring at my dog
Screeching down my door
Oh no!

Trees blown down
My dad was angry
But my mum was pleased
Tiles came off houses' roofs
Neighbours extra mad.

I love the wind
It gives me lots of fun
But I hate the wind
When it does bad things.

Grant Rankin (9)
Houston Primary School

RAIN

The rain comes,
Pitter-pattering on the window,
As it makes me think of the dropping stones,
It skitts off the windowpane
And helps the crops grow,
Although it can destroy,
By flooding houses.
When it stops, all is calm.

Craig McCowan (9)
Houston Primary School

SNOW

The cold white drop of a snowflake comes
Making a silent and gentle sound.
It makes me think of a cold white bird
Silently creeping and crawling.
The cold white flake dances and prances about.
It hopes not to be noticed or found
But then children come and step,
Make pictures with it
But eventually it disappears without a sound.

After it disappears it turns into rain with style
Pitter-pattering upon the rooftops
It hits tins and bins and cats and rats
But it has to go soon
Slowly the rain dies down,
We all put down our umbrellas
And walk down the path with a grin.

Nadine Graham (9)
Houston Primary School

WIND

The wind comes like a howling werewolf,
It whips the trees like an angry ringmaster
Then suddenly calms down to a gentle breeze.

The wind comes angrily and fiercely
Dancing and prancing through the towns and villages
Then moves on to another city.

Finlay Fraser (9)
Houston Primary School

RAINDROPS

Raindrops, raindrops
Pattering on your windowpane
Wake up in horror!
Umbrellas blowing inside out
Oh my!
Windows getting battered
Electricity wires wobbling
Lights going on and off
A monster at work
Oh my! What a day
Tiles flying everywhere
People going to work freezing cold
Everybody with scarves around their necks
Oh what a day!

Scott Campbell (9)
Houston Primary School

THE WEATHER

The hailstones come
Booming, splattering,
Smashing and spinning
Through the windowpanes
Hailstones, the size of golf balls
Smashing through your windows.
Now they're denting the tops of your roof tiles
And coming in your bedroom.
I don't really like them
Because they hurt my face
And make me cold too.

Kirsty Smith (9)
Houston Primary School

CREATURES OF THE SKY

Fog
The fog comes,
creeping slowly, inch by inch,
like a robber fresh out of a bank,
engulfing you, sucking you up,
taking you to a world of confusion,
then it moves to its next awaiting victim.

Snow
The snow comes,
plopping flake by flake,
like the clouds bursting in the sky,
covering you in a carpet of white,
creating snow graveyards everywhere.

Wind
The wind comes,
whistling everywhere,
like the world turning at hyperspeed,
pushing and slapping as it goes,
and then all is calm.

Frost
The frost comes,
cracking when it warms,
like the sun turning into a snowball,
ruling its ice kingdom
and then the heat comes back.

Alex Cameron (9)
Houston Primary School

SNOW

The snow comes at Christmas,
The snow falls as silent as a mouse.
Children rush home from school and pick a snowball fight.
We build a big, fat snowman and knock it over.
It covers the city in a big, white blanket.
Children get soaked.
They start to cry.
Snow is fun but it gets you wet.
Snow!
Snow!
Snow!
Snow!
What can we do about it?

Calum Jowett (9)
Houston Primary School

SNOW

The snow comes
Secretly, silent and gentle.
It makes you think of big, white clouds
And plain white sheets of paper.
It doesn't make a noise,
Just lies there calm and peaceful
It's just like small, little fluffy lambs
That lie on the ground too.
I like to have snowfights with my friends,
Make snowmen and angels and other things.
I take off my scarf, hat, jacket too
So I can take a nice photo of the snowman and me.

Jacolyn Kincaid (9)
Houston Primary School

SNOW

The snow comes
in its silence and calmness
making me think of a white blanket.
It crunches when you walk on it and
makes you want to stay and play.

The snow is as white as a big sheet of paper
and no one dares to write
probably if it is still there
it'll stay as white as white.

The snow comes down
softly to the ground
making me feel that
winter is coming around.

Kathryn Lindsay (9)
Houston Primary School

SNOW

The snow comes
As silent as a mouse
It lies calm on the road
It stays lying on the roof of a house
And it will stay until the rain comes
Then it will all disappear
There will be no snow on the ground
Until the next snow, there will be no sound.

Steven Kerr (9)
Houston Primary School

SNOW

The snow comes
so silent, so peaceful.
It makes my mind think of a giant Siberian tiger
spreading across the land.
It's nice and thick to build a snowman,
everybody hoping no rain shall come.
In the morning thicker snow,
children cry with laughter,
hoping the future will not come soon.
Oh the grand snow
not a blizzard I suppose.
The poor children cannot play outside.
The snowmen build a snowcastle as the snow rests
on the snowmen's hats.

Robyn Martin (9)
Houston Primary School

THE RAIN

The rain is coming,
Pitter-patter, pitter-patter goes the rain,
Bouncing off the windowpane,
Banging on the slates of houses
Like smashing plates scaring mouses,
And growing crops and flooding buildings,
Then it moves on leaving the sun to dry up the rain.
Then it begins all over again.

Brian Stephen (9)
Houston Primary School

WEATHER THAT DRIVES US MAD

The hailstones come,
They sound like a drum,
Like a giant walking through the street,
On its big, huge feet.
It bangs off the windowpane,
Smashes off the ground,
And swirls around and around.
It looks like marbles on the ground and falling from the sky.

The fog comes,
Silently and gently through the sky,
Like a blanket spreading itself out over the street,
Covering the trees and houses.
It sneaks through all the nooks and crannies,
And in through every window it finds its way!

Georgia Porch (9)
Houston Primary School

THUNDER AND LIGHTNING

The thunder comes crashing, banging and booming,
The thunder comes like a big brass band,
It booms and bangs and scares little children,
And makes shivers go down your spine.

The lightning comes sparky, bright with thunder by its side,
The lightning comes like a bulb exploding,
Flashing, crashing, and striking houses.

Emma Calvert (9)
Houston Primary School

THE WISHING BOX

There are hundreds of wishes
In my wishing box that overflows.

A sunny day
So I can go out to play,
To be a footballer
Because I could score a goal,
To fly,
To soar over the trees,
To have a dog,
So I could play with it.

We chained up my box
And threw away the key.

Gregor Preston-Jones (8)
Houston Primary School

WIND

The wind comes
Moaning, groaning, howling and roaring
It roars loudly like a shouting giant
It can blow off tiles and cause chaos
When it is over all I can see is destruction

It had smashed against the window
Like we were its greatest foe
Knocking over everything
Whistling like it's trying to sing

It won't stop until dawn
And in the morning it will move on!

Rachel Harris (8)
Houston Primary School

RAIN

The rain comes, the rain batters off the windowpane,
The rain drums like the drummer, drumming his beat,
It gets you soaked as if somebody has just thrown you into a river

The heavy rain dies down to a gentle pitter-patter, pitter-patter,
Now the gentle rain bounces off the windowpane
The rain dies and moves on to the next place.

Andrew Morrison (9)
Houston Primary School

SNOW

The snow comes down in little droplets and very peacefully.
The snow sits on the runway until it gets run over by a plane.
The snow spreads across the land like a giant white tiger.
Children cry out with laughter.
They build snowmen and igloos.
But when it rains the snow turns into slush and everyone goes home.

Fraser Jowett (9)
Houston Primary School

WIND

The wind comes like a growling beast,
It is like a whooshing rocket in the sky,
It whips at the trees continuously trying to whip them to pieces,
When it has done the damage it slowly dies and then moves on.

Craig McKissack (9)
Houston Primary School

SNOW

The snow comes slowly, silently and quietly.
The snow has no loud sound at all.
The snow is like a detective, slowly and sneakily,
Always stopping people.
The snow comes down in wavy lines like the sea.
The snow makes us laugh and have snowball fights.
That's what the snow does.

Liam Hunter (9)
Houston Primary School

SNOW

The snow comes
It makes a silent, gentle landing
Snow makes me think of snowmen
It makes us laugh and have fun
When snow finishes falling
It looks like a giant, white, cosy, warm blanket.

Lauren McCrudden (9)
Houston Primary School

THE SNOW COMES

The snow comes
down with its silent, gentle flakes,
coming, lying on the rooftops, making children shout
and then having fun
snowballs splattering across the window.

Craig Hawthorn (9)
Houston Primary School

WIND

The wind comes whooshing and whistling round our street
                                        like a white silhouette.
It made me feel anxious at the window sill
I would have rather swallowed a pill,
It made me feel ill!
Outside the flowerpots fell and cracked on the hard stone steps,
And leaves blew out of the trees like a swarm of brown flies
                                        that dived and dipped.

Douglas Webb (9)
Houston Primary School

SNOW

The snow comes down as silent as a mouse
and covers the roof of my house.
I like to see it dancing in the sky,
but it only flies aimlessly very, very high.
Now the day is over I watch the last snow tear,
that's a sign the angels are near.

Sam Jamieson (9)
Houston Primary School

THE SNOW COMES!

The snowflakes come,
The snow sounds peaceful and calm,
Like the silence in the middle of the night,
It covers the land of cold with a blanket,
And disappears later on.

Rebecca Robertson (9)
Houston Primary School

THE WIND

The wind comes
Like a growling dog,
It reminds me of a fierce, wild hog,
It blows people off their feet,
And people begin to fleet,
It blows crops out of their places,
And they all blow into people's faces,
When it's finished its damage it moves on!

Abdul Tarmal (9)
Houston Primary School

THE WIND

The wind comes,
Rushing round trees and houses,
And blowing everyone's scarves round their necks,
Howling like a werewolf when a full moon is out.
The wind can damage things,
And knock over people.
Then the wind goes away and all is calm.

Kirsty Clark (9)
Houston Primary School

THE WIND

The wind comes,
The wind is strong and mighty,
It turns umbrellas inside out
And lifts people off their feet.
It makes me think of wolves howling very loudly.

Katie Whittle (9)
Houston Primary School

THE WIND

The tree branches are broken,
The bin falls down,
The wind is howling hard against my window,
Blowing at my door,
The fences are broken down,
The windows are shaking,
The shed's blown down,
The lamp post light's off,
It is a disaster.
I like it,
The wind was making a noise,
I went back to sleep,
Newspapers flying everywhere,
Tiles flying everywhere too,
Oh no!

Naveed Rasul (9)
Houston Primary School

THE FROST

The frost comes
Silently
It covers all the grass
With a crispy layer
Of white ice.
It crawls up the stems of flowers
Making them bow low to the ground
The frost also climbs up trees
Making them like ice
Until the sun comes out
And makes it vanish.

Sarah Lyall (9)
Houston Primary School

RAIN

Rain falls like water in showers
It pitter-patters all day
I wonder why it rains because you don't get out to play
You don't get out a lot and that is boring
Some people like rain because you get wet
The rain falls out of the clouds like a cloth being squeezed.

Iona Lee (9)
Houston Primary School

SNOW

The snow comes,
It makes a gentle, soft and peaceful sound,
As it drops on the ground,
It's like a big, white blanket spread across the ground,
You could bounce on it like a white bouncy castle,
But soon it will melt.

Samantha Murray (9)
Houston Primary School

MY REMOTE-CONTROLLED CAR

My remote-controlled car
It doesn't go very far.
It goes about a quarter of a metre,
And then spills out petrol, a litre.
I hop and jump and jump and hop,
Quick! Send it back to the shop!

Alan McLean (10)
Kilbarchan Primary School

COOL

You are cool,
So, so cool,
You don't need to be funny,
So if you try to make me laugh
You don't need to be funny.

My mum says you're funny,
My dad says you're funny,
You do make me laugh
And maybe silly like a Billy!

My mum and dad don't make me laugh,
But you are so, so funny!
Nobody can make me laugh,
But you are so, so funny!

Lorne Campbell (9)
Kilbarchan Primary School

KITTENS

There they are all snuggled up,
Looking at them while I'm drinking out of a cup,
Then they look up at me,
Wanting to sit on my knee.

They are all so soft and cute,
They fall asleep when I play my flute,
As quiet as a tiny little mouse
Settled in my nice warm house.

I love it when they run so fast,
Soon they'll be zooming past.
I love my little kittens
But they stole my mittens!

Jordan Clark (9)
Kilbarchan Primary School

ALL ABOUT ME

I go to school at nine o'clock,
I'm at school for six hours,
I go home at three o'clock.

I go home and play with my friends,
I play on my bike with my friends,
I go to the shops with my friends,
I like my friends.

I live in Kilbarchan,
And I go to Kilbarchan School.
I play in Kilbarchan,
I live near a shop,
I like Kilbarchan.

Lindsey Anderson (9)
Kilbarchan Primary School

HORSES

Horses are cute,
Their tails are soft,
Put the bridle and saddle on.

Walk to the ring,
Trot round the ring,
Canter, canter, canter.

Horses are cute,
Their tails are soft,
Take the bridle and saddle off.

I love horses!

Nicole Brown (9)
Kilbarchan Primary School

SUMMER

We all wear summer hats,
Sunglasses to protect our eyes,
We buy ice cream to cool us down
In case we overheat.

After that we have a little paddle,
Splish, splash, splish, splash.

It's too warm to wear trousers
So we wear shorts and T-shirt,
Then we go for a cycle
With our dad,
And a basket trailing behind,
It has juice inside.

When we come back
We have a little fun,
We take the paddling pool out,
Then we dive in, *splash!*

Lynsey Macleod (9)
Kilbarchan Primary School

AUTUMN

I see the autumn leaves falling down, down, down,
Then people walking past hear crunch, crunch, crunch,
From the crunching leaves below their feet.

All the autumn colours,
Red, gold, orange, brown and yellow.
They are all different shapes and sizes,
So many to choose and so many to lose!

Helen Tatner (10)
Kilbarchan Primary School

FOOTBALL

I like football because I like playing it,
I am good at it.
I like it, so I can get dirty and mucky,
I can score lots of goals and save lots of shots.

I also meet friends at football,
They are good at it too.
It is sore when you get tackled,
It is really sore and sometimes you bleed.

It is really fun, football,
You get cold at first,
Then you are roasting.
I really like football
Because I score lots of goals.

Jordan Walker (9)
Kilbarchan Primary School

SUMMER

It's summer again and an enjoyable time,
We hope the weather's going to be nice,
The paddling pool is nice and cool,
We all want an enjoyable summer
And not one where there will be rain!

It's the end of school, hooray!
I get home and watch TV.
I don't want the summer to end
Because I want the sun
And the summer all the time!

Laura McCracken (10)
Kilbarchan Primary School

THE FLUFFY DOGS

Dogs are fluffy and loud,
And fast and furry too, thirsty and hungry sometimes.
Some are fat, thin or big with big, sharp teeth.
They have waggly tails, some wear coats.

With thin, little feet, some have big, fat bodies
With hair all over it everywhere.
They get taken for walks every day
By their owners.

They have to be trained if they want the lead off.
Some are puppies, others are bigger,
Some are giant and some take sticks!

Darren Andrew (9)
Kilbarchan Primary School

ALL ABOUT MY FRIEND

We make a very good friendship
Because we nearly always go
Out with each other.

She is very kind,
And very helpful, my friend.
She has a very kind mum and dad,
We even go to see Meghan and Mitchell.

We are very gentle to each other,
I am very nice to her,
And she is very nice to me,
I have a very nice friend!

Laura Ross (9)
Kilbarchan Primary School

THE MILKY BAR CREME EGG

The Milky Bar Creme Egg
Is so yummy, it has creamy orange stuff inside it,
it is chocolatey as well,
It is very refreshing on a hot summer's day.

It is pale white on the outside,
But on the inside it
Is bright orange!

It is scrumptious and bright
And it is nice,
Nice, nice.
It is so nice,
It is impossible to explain how good it tastes.

Grant Marshall (9)
Kilbarchan Primary School

BONFIRE NIGHT

I see bright colours rising,
Exploding in the sky.

I hear the banging as they
Explode up high.

I smell the wood burning
As the guy sits on the flames.

I feel the warmth of the bonfire,
That keeps me warm outside.

Katryn Stuart (10)
Kilbarchan Primary School

MATHS

Go to maths and get my jotter, pencil and ruler,
I start to write in my jotter,
Then I have finished.

Getting the sums off the whiteboard,
After that when I am finished
I take it out to the teacher.

Then my teacher marks it
And if they are right she tells me to put it away,
Or if they are wrong
I have to go and correct them.

I go and get my maths folder
And finish things off,
Like my three times table searches.
I love maths.

Lauren Hyndman (9)
Kilbarchan Primary School

AUTUMN

Falling, tumbling, that's what they do,
They're turning yellow, red, orange too.
They crunch as over them you walk and run,
These are the signs that tell you autumn has begun.

Our summer memories are fading back,
But it's not yet time for Santa's sack.
It's a time in the middle, it's what we call
Autumn, autumn when leaves fall.

Autumn makes us happy and cheerful,
It does not make you sad and tearful.
Your leaves are now lying on the ground,
Your yellow, orange and red leaves are finally down!

Sarah Dyer (10)
Kilbarchan Primary School

MY DOG

My dog is black and brown,
He always wants a cuddle
Every now and then.
Once he's had a bath
He's really, really fluffy.
When he barks
It's really loud, like a lion.

When you go to bed
He always bites your foot,
Because he wants a cuddle
Every now and then.

When I wake up
He comes and licks my head,
So I get up or else
As he wants a cuddle
Every now and then.

My dog is a man-eater,
But I give him a cuddle
Every now and then,
I love my dog.

Christine Cameron (8)
Kilbarchan Primary School

FOOTBALL CRAZY

Football is fun, so much to do,
Even scoring a goal is hard.
When you come to think of it,
Maybe not but I don't think so.
When we score it is a lot of fun,
But when we lost a goal
It gets simply boring.

When we hit the goalpost
We wish they weren't there.
When we hit the goalpost
And it goes in
We wish they were there.
When the goalie's bored
We are scared when he comes out of goal.

When the football's round
We wish there wasn't one visible.
We wish they weren't around
But when it trips us up
And it gives us a penalty
We like it very much!

Ryan McKellar (9)
Kilbarchan Primary School

COLD WEATHER

I feel the freezing snow in my hands,
I see the icicles hanging from the roof,
I go very fast on the ice and I feel like an angel,
I see the steam coming out of my mouth,
It's now winter.

Elspeth Chalmers (10)
Kilbarchan Primary School

HORSE

Check the girth, then up I go,
Thud! Ouch, that was sore,
Then the teacher says to go with the flow,
Stirrups fixed two twists to the top.

Walk on,
Walking forward to the track,
Then just check the horse's back.
Head up, back straight,
Watching the steps I make,
Round the school once then . . .

Trotting along the muddy track,
Up down, up down,
Up I go,
Thinking this is fun,
Over the trotting poles,
One, two, three,
Then back to walk.

Then the teacher says to turn in,
Uh oh!
This means we're going to canter over jumps,
I'm scared.
I'm first,
I go out to the track then ask . . .
Canter.

Lauren White (9)
Kilbarchan Primary School

BROWNIES

Brownies is fun, great and fab,
But sometimes it is bad,
If you fall off your bed,
And crack your head,
Then you have to stay in bed.

Then next Friday when you go,
Everyone says, 'Hello, hello.'
Then when it gets hot and stuffy,
That's when you want to go,
But Brownies is fun, great and fab,
(That's why we all say no, no, no!)

Then when the time comes to say goodbye,
We all say don't cry so then we stop,
And rest our heads on our warm and soft bed.

Hollie Porteous (9)
Kilbarchan Primary School

SCHOOL

School, school is cool,
Because you get to use felt-tip pens,
And get to play football and go to the gym.

I like school because of that,
And a whole bunch of other stuff too.

You've got to know you're never alone in school,
And that's what makes it really cool,
Because . . . it just is!

Mark Docherty (9)
Kilbarchan Primary School

LUIGE

Luige is his name,
A hairy ball of fluff,
With a tiny face and nose,
Wandering about the farm he goes.

When I am eating a sweet
He comes and sits at my feet,
Staring up into my face,
My dog is *ace!*

David Seymour (9)
Kilbarchan Primary School

THE MOON

The moon
Glimmers
Like a jewel in a crown,
Moves
Like a snail along the ground,
Glistens
Like a star twinkling,
Smiles
Like a child on Christmas morning,
Shines
Like a World Cup,
Gleams
Like a small, clear icicle.

Victoria Smith (8)
Langbank Primary School

MY HOUSE

Above my house
is a never-ending
rainbow sparkling
as shiny as the
crown jewels.

Below my house
are the secrets of
the dead where
people once lived
long, long ago.

Around my house
is a crooked old
fence where the
cows itch their
backs on a
hot summer's day

Beside my house
is a dark green
field where
the cows eat
and eat at the
grass every day.

Inside my house
is my arguing little
brother who never
shuts up when Mum
and Dad tell him.

Beyond my house
is my farming future
where I will buy all
the modern machinery.

Callum MacRae (9)
Langbank Primary School

MY HOUSE

Above my house
are fluffy white
clouds like woolly sheep
and a sky as blue as a
pool of cool water
and the sun as
bright as a
winning goal.

Below my house
there are secrets
long ago that are
only known to the
underground bugs
and roots from trees
that swirl and curl
like a classic
Roberto Carlos
free kick.

Beside my house
there are old trees
with mossy trunks
and branches giving
homes to small
creatures.

Over my house
is a rainbow
as colourful as
a paintbox and
the birds who
sing all day.

Tom Ellis (9)
Langbank Primary School

MY HOUSE

Above my house
is the bright blue
sky and the clouds
as fluffy as candyfloss
and a rainbow
as colourful as rainbow trout.

Beside my house
is a crooked old shed
and a wobbly old wall
where I crashed
my bike!

Below my house
is a dark cave
where cavemen
lived and the roots
of the big tree.

Around my house
is an old wire fence
and an old broken tree.

Over my house
is a great big tree
where birds nest
and lay their eggs.

Inside my house
is my prized
possession, my
family who
mess about all
the time.

Beyond my house
is my future,
my amazing,
fun future.

Duncan Fletcher (9)
Langbank Primary School

WHY? WHY? WHY?

The milkman, every time the milkman comes,
Away go the cats, bark goes the dog,
Why? Why? Why does the milkman come?

I don't know, I don't know, go and ask your daddy O.

The postman, every time the postman comes,
Rattle goes the letterbox, squeak goes the bird,
Why? Why? Why does the postman come?

I don't know, I don't know, go and ask your granny O.

The paperboy, every time the paperboy comes,
Whack goes the paper on my daddy's head,
Why? Why? Why does the paperboy come?

I don't know, I don't know, go and ask your papa O.

The teacher, every time the teacher yells,
'Oh no,' go the kids,
'Here goes my voice,' says the teacher,
Why? Why? Why does the teacher yell?

I don't know, I don't know, go and ask your teacher O.

Why? Why? Why do teachers always yell?

I know, I know, you behave badly.

Simon Beveridge (11)
Langbank Primary School

MY HOUSE

Above my house
is a shining sun
bright as can be.

Over my house
is a rainbow
as colourful as
a paintbox.

Inside my house is
my noisy sister,
as noisy as a
jumbo jet.

Beside my house
is the stony,
rocky garden wall.

Around my house
is a green garden,
green as a blob of
paint that has been
splodged on.

Beside my house
is the train track,
as noisy as a
baby's cry.

Beyond my house
are more houses
belonging to my friends.

Below my
house is the
afterlife of
ancient civilisation.

Daniel Keegan (9)
Langbank Primary School

I WISH . . .

I wish I could fly,
Up into the sky.
I wish I had a car
So I could drive to the stars,
I wish, I wish, I wish.

I wish I could see
What will happen to me,
And what about my family?
I wish, I wish, I wish.

I wish I could sail across the sea,
Nobody else but me.
I wish I had sweets
And pleats in my hair,
I wish, I wish, I wish.

I wish I could do and have
All these things,
And many, many more.

Laura Mitchell (11)
Langbank Primary School

PUDDLES

The rain comes splashing down,
Landing on the ground,
Flowing all around,
Making puddles.

Out come the children
Making lots of noise,
Playing with their toys,
Jumping in the puddles.

When the puddles rise
They spread wide,
Right out to every side,
Bigger and bigger are the puddles.

Flowing in rivers,
Turning into vapour,
Looking like paper,
Away go the puddles.

Changing into clouds,
Getting heavier all the time,
Falling as fast as a rhyme,
There go the puddles.

The rain comes falling down,
Landing on the ground,
Flowing all around,
Making puddles.

Emma Gilchrist (11)
Langbank Primary School

MY HOUSE IN LANGBANK

Above my house
are lots of fluffy clouds
floating across the
sky like floating sheep
in a field.

Beside my house is
a bright blue
Beetle car as
blue as the ocean.

Below my house
is where the Devil
lives, red devils as
red as hot boiling lava.

Around my house
are lots of plants,
plants as pink as
ballet shoes, as
green as a pot
of paint,
as blue as the
sky itself.

Inside my house
is my dog, as crazy as
a person that has got something
that they'd wanted.

Beyond my house
are my friends who
will stay with me forever.

That is my house.

Samantha Campbell (9)
Langbank Primary School

THE MOON

The moon
reflects
like a golden coin,
shines
like a star that the Three Wise Men followed,
spins
like a spinning top, round it goes,
glows
like a child smiling,
brings brightness
like a sun just polished,
lights the sky
like a firework so high.

Bruce Abernethy (8)
Langbank Primary School

THE MOON

The moon
shines
like a diamond on a ring,
glistens
like a bauble on a Christmas tree,
reflects
like a mirror,
gleams
like a star,
moves
like a little, slow tortoise,
changes
like a caterpillar coming out of a cocoon.

Jacqueline Hamilton (8)
Langbank Primary School

ABOVE AND BELOW

Above my house
are the singing blackbirds,
like the singing of a choir.

Beside my house
is a tall, green tree,
as tall as a giant's house.

Below my house
is the disgusting stuff,
bones, spiders and worms.

Around my house
is the lovely bright flowers,
as bright as the sun.

Suzy Hansen (9)
Langbank Primary School

THE MOON

The moon glistens
like a jewel in the sky.
The moon gleams
like a brass button in a sea of stars.
The moon moves
like a piece of metal going to Mars.
The moon spins
like a spinning top on stars.
The moon glimmers
like a midnight star.
The moon smiles
like a child on Christmas Day.

Charlotte Linn (8)
Langbank Primary School

MY HOUSE

Above my house
is the sky as blue as a tub of paint,
and as unpredictable as the sea.
The clouds as fluffy as candyfloss
and a rainbow as colourful as a paintbox,
and that is what's above my house.

Inside my house
is a family which nobody dares to go near,
they are as grumpy as bulls and have pig ears,
and snort like pigs every night and day,
and I am the only kind one who everyone loves,
and that is what is inside my house.

Below my house is the unknown dead
and dinosaur bones from years ago.
The tree roots are like spiders webs
and secrets are unknown under there
where the worms are dead
and where ants are busy getting food
and that is what's below my house.

Ian Gunn (9)
Langbank Primary School

THE MOON

The moon glistens like a snowball,
Shines like a shooting star,
Changes like an apple changes colour,
Glimmers like my pink bedroom light,
Smiles like a girl or boy at Christmas,
Glows like a candle on a cake.

Beth Fraser (8)
Langbank Primary School

MY HOUSE

Above my house
is the big blue sky,
the sun as bright as the summer,
and the rainbow as colourful as a paintbox,
the clouds as fluffy as sheep
and the sky as blue as the sea.

Below my house
are the secrets of the deep,
the spiders, the worms and snails,
the house of the Neanderthal who lived long ago,
the devils who live below.

Beside my house
are the dark, creepy woods,
the woods as dark as dungeons.
Beside my house
are my neighbours who are never ever in,
if they get letters they chuck them in the bin.

Adam Saunders (9)
Langbank Primary School

THE MOON

The moon glows like a flying saucer in space,
Looks like there's a man on the moon smiling,
Shines like a river in the night,
Reflects like a mirror in a bright night,
Moves like an alien dancing in the sky,
Smiling like a snowman in a snowstorm.

Daniel Morgan (8)
Langbank Primary School

MY HOUSE

Above my house is the
sky as blue as the sea,
and the clouds as fluffy as
sheep and candyfloss,
and all the birds as quiet as mice,
also a rainbow as colourful
as the newborn day.

Below my house
is the dark, mysterious cave where
the dead once lived,
and also soil and earth
as soft as my pillow.

Inside my house
is a howling family,
in my house they
are as secret as fairies
and my bed is a garden town.

Jamie Hookham (9)
Langbank Primary School

THE MOON

The moon shines like a jewel in a sea of stars,
Glows like a black night sky,
Gleams like a chest full of treasure,
Smiles like you or I on Christmas Day.
The moon also sings a song like a little bird cheeping,
But the moon helps us to have light on a cold and wintry night.

Lynsey Mackay (8)
Langbank Primary School

THE FARM

On the farm
There are lots of things,
Drive an old, slow tractor,
Speed on a zooming quad.

On the farm
There are lots of things,
Big, friendly sheep,
Small, shy lambs.

On the farm
There are lots of things,
Jump and skid on your bike,
Run, throw the grass after it is cut.

I'm happy on my farm,
That is why I love my *farm!*

Gregor Fletcher (11)
Langbank Primary School

MY HOUSE

Above my house there is the sky as untold
as the sea, with clouds as fluffy as candyfloss.

Beside my house is my garden with flowers
and trees and my mum gardening as busy as a bee.

Below my house is the earth, knowing secrets
of the prehistoric past.

Inside my house is my very annoying, pestering sister.

Beyond my house are the hills, full of sheep and grass
like green paint trapped on the hill.

Calum McFarlane (8)
Langbank Primary School

THE MOON

The moon
gleams
like a World Cup,
shines
like a star,
glows
like a sun,
moves
like a slug,
smiles
like a child getting their photo,
spins
like an alien in a spaceship.

Andrew Smith (8)
Langbank Primary School

THE MOON

The moon
moves
like a very slow tortoise,
gleams
like a star in the dark night,
changes
like a chameleon,
smiles
like a chain of stars,
shines
like the sun,
glows
like fire.

Andrew Galt (8)
Langbank Primary School

THE MOON

The moon
glistens
like a copper coin,
Glows
like a bit of ice on the ground,
Changes
like a human's face,
Moves
like a butterfly in the sky,
Shines
like a star in the night,
Brings brightness
like a spark.

Kenneth Rocke (8)
Langbank Primary School

THE MOON

The moon shines
like a pot of silver,
looks
like a merry person,
glows
like a lamp,
moves
like a floating football,
changes
like a chameleon,
glistens
like a roll of tinsel.

Daniel MacRae (8)
Langbank Primary School

The Moon

The moon shines like a shining star,
Glistens like Christmas baubles,
Changes like an apple,
Smiles like a child's face on Christmas Day,
Glows like a polished necklace,
Moves like a snail.

Suzanne Robertson (8)
Langbank Primary School

The Moon

The moon gleams like a clean plate,
Glimmers like a diamond in the sun,
Glistens like a star in the sky,
Glows like a penny under the light,
Moves like the wind going softly,
Shines like my heart-shaped mirror.

Fern Fletcher (8)
Langbank Primary School

The Moon

The moon shines like a shining star,
Gleams like a polished stone,
Glows like a light,
Glistens like a lake at night,
Smiles like a child's face,
Changes like a clock's face.

Naomi Le Sage (8)
Langbank Primary School

MY HOUSE

Above my house
is a sky as bright
as gold
and clouds
as soft as candyfloss.

Beside my house is
a gate as black as
the night.

Below my house
are the mysteries of
life and the Earth's core.

Inside my house
is my sister as
annoying as fleas.

Beyond my house
is my future yet
unwoven.

Euan Wilkie (9)
Langbank Primary School

THE MOON

The moon glistens like a piece of gold in the night sky,
Moves like a star steered by a cloud,
Changes like a caterpillar to a beautiful butterfly,
Glows like a diamond ring in the dark,
Reflects like a glass mirror,
Smiles like a princess.

Jennifer Burns (8)
Langbank Primary School

THE MOON

The moon
glows
like a jewel glistening in the midnight sky,
spins
like a spinning top spun by a child,
reflects
like a cat's eye stuck in the road,
glimmers
like a bit of glitter stuck on a card,
moves
like a turtle wearing roller skates,
shines
like a mirror in the sky.

Jennifer Gilchrist (8)
Langbank Primary School

THE MOON

The moon
glows
like a creamy, yellowy diamond in the sky,
changes
like a Jaffa Cake as you eat it,
smiles
like a child on his birthday,
gleams
like an icicle hanging from the sky.
The moon is
like a pumpkin all round and orange,
shines
like an angel's halo floating above her head.

Louise Wallwork (8)
Langbank Primary School

COLOURS

Black
Black sky
Black sky with lovely twinkling stars

Red
Red love
Red love is wonderful
It's good when someone loves you

Green
Green juicy
Green juicy apples are good for you.

Cheryl Sanderson (10)
Mossvale Primary School

AT SCHOOL

I like my teacher
She is great
She gives me hard work
I love it, especially maths
I love it!

Ian Michie (8)
Mossvale Primary School

THE BEACH

The wind blowing
The sea splashing on the rocks
Seagulls flying, ducks quacking
Happiness.

Shaun Sleeth (8)
Mossvale Primary School

BONFIRE NIGHT

I hear screaming rockets soaring into the still, black sky
I hear rockets lunging into the air and cartwheels flickering.
I see flashing sparks leaping and dancing from the blazing fire
I see fireworks blasting into the very starry sky.
I smell burning embers, the charred wood and the pungent smoke
I smell the flaming fire crackling wood and think how good it is.
I taste sweet, melting marshmallows singed on the fork tips
I taste the crispy chicken leg on my tender lips
I feel the warmth from the fire setting my face aglow.

David Yates (11)
Mossvale Primary School

REMEMBRANCE

R   emember the people who died in the world
E   veryone was sorry for the soldiers
M   ichael Jackson sang 'Heal The World' to make people think
E   vil grows in the world
M   en try to make peace but no luck
B   ombs bang and destroy life
E   ach day is frightening in war
R   oaring battles devastate the world.

Steven Sim (11)
Mossvale Primary School

COLOURS

Blue
Blue sea
Blue sea sparkling in the summer sun

Orange
Orange sun
Orange sun in the light blue sky

Mint
Mint chocolate
Mint chocolate, sweet and delicious

Purple
Purple grapes
Purple grapes, all juice and scrumptious.

Danielle D'Arcy (10)
Mossvale Primary School

REMEMBRANCE DAY

R emember the soldiers who died in the bloody battle.
E veryone died for us to live in peace.
M any people of the war died.
E vil was a murdering thing for them.
M en were marching through the marshes.
B lood, a murdering time for the soldiers.
E ach soldier had their own gun and bullets.
R eally all the soldiers would return some day,
   the rest would never come back.

Michael Steele (11)
Mossvale Primary School

TRAGEDY IN NEW YORK

I was affected by the fact
That people would kill one another,
I think the world should get along together,
When I heard it hit, I thought,
How did this happen? Who did this disgusting thing?
I thought America was invincible!

Stuart Sleeth (10)
Mossvale Primary School

PUMPKINS

P umpkins are scary things
U gly skeletons in the dark
M umbling witches in the sky
P itch-black scary nights
K iller witches out at night
I n the night the vampire bats come out
N ibbling necks!

Jane Campbell (8)
Mossvale Primary School

THE GARDEN

The garden is a wonderful place to be
A really adventurous place for me
I can eat a lovely bun
And also have lots of fun
Then it is time to go in the house
To feed my little pet mouse.

Chloe Lupton (8)
Mossvale Primary School

FOOTBALL

I see the ball in the air
I hear people shouting
I smell the food from the burger van
I head the ball into the goal
Everybody cheers!

William Yates (8)
Mossvale Primary School

PUMPKIN

P   umpkin soup
U   nmade
M um eats
P   umpkin soup
K ind of horrible
I   n the bin pumpkin goes
N ever eat that pumpkin soup again.

Rachel Flynn (8)
Mossvale Primary School

PUMPKINS

P   umpkins, cats and big black bats
U   gly ghosts hover in the night
M ice and spiders
P   umpkins, rats
K iller witches out tonight
I   'm a witch with the scariest face
N ight of fright!

Ashlee Waton (8)
Mossvale Primary School

SHABBAT

Candles flickering
Mum's blessing
Smell of the bread, mmm
Good time with our family.

Steven Pollock (8)
Mossvale Primary School

THE MAGIC MOUSE

I saw a magic mouse one day
He had a pointy hat,
He hopped on a train
And went down the lane.
He came back the next week
With all his magic kit.
He got out his wand
And said something funny.
With a swish and a poke and a puff of smoke
He vanished into thin air
And he flew away on that very sunny day.

David Kerr (8)
Mossvale Primary School

BONFIRE NIGHT

I hear screaming rockets soaring into the still, black sky
I hear the ear-bursting screech of the bangers.
I see flashing sparks leaping and dancing from the blazing fire.
I see the shining flame of Superman ready to blast-off.
I smell the burning embers, the charred wood and the pungent smoke.
I smell powdery flares that came from exploding rockets in the night.
I taste sweet, melting marshmallows singed on the fork tips.
I taste the burgers burning in the barbecue.
I feel the warmth from the fire setting my face aglow.

Steven Dunsmore (11)
Mossvale Primary School

GREEN

Green
Green grass
Green grass blowing in the garden
Like a gentle whisper.

Green
Green apples
Green apples brighten up the trees
Like the lights on the Christmas tree.

Green
Green leaves
Green leaves swaying in the breeze
Like in springtime.

Emma Harper (10)
Mossvale Primary School

BLUE

Blue
Blue waves
Blue waves crashing wildly against the rocks.

Blue
Blue balloon
Blue balloon swaying away up into the sky.

Blue
Blue sky
Blue sky covered by the white cotton wool clouds.

Frazer Macdonald
Mossvale Primary School

COLOURS

Blue,
Blue waves,
Blue waves crashing against the ragged rocks.

Green,
Green grass,
Green grass swaying from side to side.

White,
White snow,
White snow soaking into your skin.

Yellow,
Yellow sun,
Yellow sun shining beautifully in the sky.

Orange,
Orange octopus,
Orange octopus floating in the sea.

Stuart Caldwell (9)
Mossvale Primary School

HAPPINESS

Happiness is blue
it tastes like sweets
and it smells like fresh air.
Happiness looks like fresh grass
and it sounds like birds singing.
Happiness feels like a new world.

Ashleigh McMichael (10)
Mossvale Primary School

COLOURS

Blue
Blue waves
Blue waves crashing against the craggy rocks.

Red
Red love
Red love booming against the loved heart.

Purple
Purple fish
Purple fish swimming across the deep blue sea.

Orange
Orange star
Orange star upon the darkest sky.

Strawberry
Strawberry tart
Strawberry tart so nice and creamy.

Daniella Gallacher (9)
Mossvale Primary School

REMEMBER

R   emember the soldiers who have battles
E   nduring the hardship of the war
M   any men are marching cold, frightened and alone
E   vil people are bombing the country
M   any people who are bloody and dying
B   ullets and bombs have been getting let off
E   very soldier is helping one another
R   emember your family is missing you.

Amanda Craig (11)
Mossvale Primary School

COLOURS

Blue
Blue the sky
Blue the sky making shadows in the water.

Green
Green apples
Green apples are nice and juicy.

Pink
Pink bubblegum
Pink bubblegum is very chewy.

Black
Black cola
Black cola is very fizzy.

Red
Red strawberries
Red strawberries are very scrumptious.

Gold
Gold coins
Gold coins are very shiny.

Brown
Brown chocolate
Brown chocolate is very creamy.

Charlotte Taylor (10)
Mossvale Primary School

EGYPT

Egypt is a happy place
The people are nice to you.
When the pharaohs die
It's time to mummify.

Put them in their coffin and put them in a tomb.
Booby traps are set.
If robbers come they'll be caught in a net
So don't come to my tomb or else you'll die.

Rachael Pringle (8)
Mossvale Primary School

REMEMBER

R emember, remember the wars of the past
E veryone who died in the wars, the poppies are
the colour of their blood
M arching men trudging through the marshy fields
E veryone who took bullets bravely
M any men and women were murdered in the wars
B lood is red and so are poppies
E veryone will be missing their partners
R emember, remember the 11th of November.

Michael McMaster (11)
Mossvale Primary School

WORLD WAR II

In World War II the bombs did drop.
The guns were fired and lives were lost.

The British fought against Hitler's men
Who attacked our country again and again.

Hitler was a nasty man, he killed thousands of Jews
But when he met with British troops, he knew that he would lose.

James Campbell (11)
Mossvale Primary School

REMEMBER

R emember those who died
E very one of them died from evil around the world
M illions of men murdered
E ach of them sacrificed their lives
M iserable families around the world
B lood streams upon the site
E xplosions fill the air
R ed poppies for life.

Lauren Coyle (11)
Mossvale Primary School

AMERICAN TRAGEDY

I hope they have a better future.
I hope they all make up.
I hope they pray for the people who died.
I hope they build the Trade Center again.
I hope they don't let it happen again.

Nicole Wilson (10)
Mossvale Primary School

HOPE

I hoped the American flag would stand
But now they need a helping hand.
The towers fell
And I hope this war will end.

Kieran Whiteford (10)
Mossvale Primary School

REMEMBER

R eady for war, the soldiers stomp out to the airfield,
E ach and every bunker left with bloodshed all over.
M en shouting for medics to help their wounds.
E verybody's emptiness at the horror of war.
M arching to their fatal deaths.
B odies on the ground.
E xposure to fear and war.
R emember them.

Sean Kelly (11)
Mossvale Primary School

REMEMBER

R emember each and
E veryone who died for us
M illions of them who were injured
E ven the traitors who
M urdered a lot of the
B ritish army and all those who
E ndured the hard life of the war
R emember all of them.

Craig Mackenzie (11)
Mossvale Primary School

HOPE

H ope is something you should never give up on.
O pportunities in school allow me to hope.
P eople have hope in each other.
E veryone should have hope.

Christopher McShane (10)
Mossvale Primary School

REMEMBRANCE

R emember the men who marched away and are still remembered
to this very day.

E veryone hates the war, too much blood and filled with gore.

M en screaming for mercy, some calling for medics,
some already dead.

E mbers burning on camp fires, some looking for rations.

M en running from murdering enemies, people being tortured
beyond belief.

B ullets flying in the air, men bleeding to death in fear.

E very battle is horrifying, planes flying overhead,
blasting guns down below.

R ed blood flowing down like a stream, men look and start to scream.

Mark Wyllie (11)
Mossvale Primary School

SENSES

My favourite sounds are the water rippling down a waterfall,
a baby laughing and a cat purring gently.
My favourite smells are petrol in a petrol station,
birthday candles just been blown out and a Chinese meal.
My favourite sights are the sun setting, small babies and kittens.
My favourite tastes are warm homemade lentil soup, Margarita
stuffed-crust pizza out of Pizza Hut and strawberries and
whipped cream.
I like to touch silk, baby's skin and comfy covers on my bed.
My best feeling is excitement.

Sarah Chalk (11)
Mossvale Primary School

DAVID SLOAN'S ACROSTIC POEM

D aring
A dventurous
V igorous
I mpatient
D izzy

S mart
L azy
O ccupied
A rtistic
N oisy.

David Sloan (10)
Mossvale Primary School

THE PARK

Swings swinging
Mum laughing
The smell of hot dogs
Tasting delicious
I feel happy.

Kirsty Kent (8)
Mossvale Primary School

HOPE

I hope there is not a World War III
I hope this will end happily
I hope there will be peace in the future
I hope people's families are okay
I hope there will be no suffering.

Christopher Logan (10)
Mossvale Primary School

BONFIRE NIGHT

I hear screaming rockets soaring into the still, black sky
I hear blazing bright fireworks scorching through as they cry
I see flashing sparks leaping and dancing from the blazing fire
I see shooting Catherine wheels revolving as they flicker and splutter
I smell the burning embers, the charred wood and the pungent smoke
I smell the shining flares as they crash to the ground
I taste sweet, melting marshmallows singed on the fork tips
I taste the crunchy chicken from the barbecue
I feel the warmth from the fire setting my face aglow.

Lee Jones (11)
Mossvale Primary School

THE NIGHTMARES OF SHOPPING

Walking round the High Street shopping
Dragging my feet along the ground, shopping
Tired and worn out by shopping
Your feet are sore
You are very tired
Then
The wind starts, your shopping is blown about.
Then
Rain! Your new jumper's getting soaked,
Your hair is being blown in the wind,
Then
Thunder strikes.
Running along with your hair in the air,
Trying to find shelter.
What a nightmare, just to go *shopping!*

Melanie McMaster (10)
Rashielea Primary School

BOB THE BUILDER'S WINTER

Winter's here, so let's get busy
The yard needs tidying, I must find Dizzy.

Roley's here and Lofty too
It's easy to tidy when there's a few of you.

Wendy's here to help me out
'Christmas is coming!' we all shout.

Our work is done, so we all say
'Hurry for the Christmas holiday.'

One more job before we rest
Decorate a tree to look the best.

Now let's rest and have some fun
Our winter jobs have all been done.

Abbie Rose Shepherd (8)
Rashielea Primary School

WHEN I WENT TO VISIT MY SISTER IN SPACE!

When I went to visit my sister in space
I looked at her closely
She had a *funny* face
She had three arms and sixteen legs
And hanging from her ears were two clothes pegs
So I went to play with my sister
I looked at her nose
And it had a big blister
Look at the time, have to go
I'll see you later, cheerio!

Siobhan McHugh (8)
Rashielea Primary School

FOOD EVERYWHERE

There's biscuits crushed in the chair
There's chocolate on the stairs
Whenever you look up at the ceiling
There's carrots floating in mid-air
There's apple mushed on the floor
Whenever Pamela takes a snack
There's food everywhere!

Hayley Walsh (8)
Rashielea Primary School

FOOD EVERYWHERE

There's carrots on my trousers
And porridge on the wall
There's potatoes on her chair
And apples on her top
Whenever Abbie eats her food
It gets everywhere!

Jordan Scott (8)
Rashielea Primary School

FOOD EVERYWHERE!

There's egg on the ceiling
There's toast on the floor
There's jam on the chair
Whenever Gran makes my food
There's food everywhere!

Emily Smith (8)
Rashielea Primary School

MESSY ERIN

There's Barbies on the bed
Spaghetti dolls on the floor
There's stickers on the ceiling
And Lego next to the door
There's Barbie clothes on the desk
And a Poo-Chi on the chair
Whenever Erin plays in her room
There's toys everywhere!

Megan McLellan (8)
Rashielea Primary School

MY DOG

My dog is strong
My dog is spotty
My dog loves toast
My dog hates the hoover
My dog cries a lot
So I cuddle him most.

Matthew Ferguson (9)
Rashielea Primary School

MY BEST FRIEND AIMEE

She has blonde hair which is like the sun
Her eyes are as blue as the sea
She is a very, very cheery person
And is always there for me
She will always be my best friend
Aimee.

Robyn Jade Agnew (10)
Rashielea Primary School

FEELINGS

All alone in my room
Lonely and sad, feeling doon
On my own every day
Nobody asking me to come and play
Everyone having fun except me on my own

Fun, fun, fun, fun
Up and down, all around
Nobody's down in the dumps

Truly joyful
I'm with my friends
Me and Mum we're having fun
Everyone's happy, don't speak too soon
I need to go to change my cousin's nappy.

Stephanie Murtagh (8)
Rashielea Primary School

THE FROGS

My friend has a frog called Freddy
I have one called Eddy
Eddy's green and yellow
And his belly feels like jello
Freddy is black and brown
My friend even made him a crown
They can do tricks
Like double forward flips
Freddy and Eddy are really good mates
They even try to find each other dates.

Martin Hughes (10)
Rashielea Primary School

MY PETS

My dog Casey looks really fat
But she's really like a cat
When you let her out in the sun
She just lies at the door like a bun.

My guinea pig Cuddles is really shy
But my other one Bubbles is like a fly
One of them is quite fat
But the other is more like a rat.

My hamster Crystal
Has always liked Bristol
She's very small
And likes her ball.

These are my pets
And I'm glad to have them.

Steven Andrew Boyd (10)
Rashielea Primary School

PEPSI

Six months old is my pup
She never stops jumping up
Chairs and beds she likes best
One time I caught her chewing my vest
Pepsi is her name, ruby is her colour
When she wants to be petted, she goes to my mother
Red is her collar to match her lead
The thing she likes best is getting her feed.

Emma Mackay (8)
Rashielea Primary School

MY PET DINOSAUR

I have a pet dinosaur
Though no one believes me
I tell them I do
Still no one believes me.

My pet dinosaur lives under my bed
He's blue and fluffy
With a pink, queer tail
A very rare type you know.

I met him on holiday
With a polar bear
A very scary bear
He nearly ate me.

He rescued me
So I took him home
And now we are best friends.

Rebecca Cottis (10)
Rashielea Primary School

WEATHER

W indy weather
E njoyable weather
A nnoying weather
T errible weather
H appy weather
E nviable weather
R ainy weather.

Ross Donaldson (10)
Rashielea Primary School

THE BRIGHT BLUE BIRD

The bright blue bird
The bright blue bird
With a chest the colour of lemon curd
The bright blue bird
The bright blue bird
Eyes that glow a bright, bright yellow
Oh! The bright blue bird
The bright blue bird
With a chest the colour of lemon curd
Eyes that glow a bright, bright yellow
Its beautiful colours flow through
The bright blue bird.

Kerry Harding (10)
Rashielea Primary School

BEST FRIEND

B   is for best friend
E   is for everlasting friendship
S   is for special friends
T   is for getting in trouble

F   is for funny times
R   is for her rabbit who is a troublesome bunny
I   is for intelligent that she is
E   is for being ever so nice to me
N   is for never being nasty
D   is for don't ruin your friendship.

Rebecca O'Neill (10)
Rashielea Primary School

MY BEST FRIEND

My best friend is Steven Boyd
He hates it when people call him Lloyd
Doesn't like to tidy up
But loves it when he's throwing up.

He likes to act like a silly clown
When nobody laughs it makes him frown
At home he acts just the same
He might even break a windowpane.

Stuart Lindsay (10)
Rashielea Primary School

MY BED

My bed is really comfy and it's double too
I don't like getting out of it
It's lovely and warm too
It's just too hard to resist
I wish my mum knew that
So every morning she wouldn't have to tell me to get up.

Alison Baldacci (10)
Rashielea Primary School

DREAMS

Sometimes you dream about big monsters
Sometimes you dream about things that make you scream
Sometimes you dream about ice cream
Dreams can be good or bad
But you will always end up back in your bed.

Aimee Calderwood (10)
Rashielea Primary School

MY BEST FRIEND

My best friend is tall and thin
My best friend has legs like pins
My best friend is always sleepy
My best friend is sometimes creepy
My best friend is always kind
My best friend has a good mind.
Which takes her a long time to unwind.

Emma Chalk (10)
Rashielea Primary School

TELEVISION

My family think it is their God
When it is only a little box
They fight over the remote control
To get it they all have a vote
A war is usually made
All over a silly little box!

Matthew Keating (10)
Rashielea Primary School

MR KELLY

My name is Mr Kelly
And I live in New Dehli
I'm watching the telly
Though my feet are very smelly
Because I was working in the garden with my wellies.

Graeme Alexander (10)
Rashielea Primary School

THE PUPPY THAT SOARED

The young little puppy wanted to travel,
He wanted to travel to Mars.
He crept into the yard,
Whipped out a card.
Started to read it silently
He jumped into the car
And said very quietly 'To Mars!'
The engine roared as the car started to move,
It left a huge groove in the grass
And it was off!
Off to Mars, the little car flew
It flew too far
And in the car, the puppy was no more
He decided to soar,
Soar away and soar in space for ever more!

Gary Stevenson (10)
Rashielea Primary School

SUNNY THE DOG

Sunny is the name of my neighbour's dog
He likes to sniff trees and logs
He always barks at night
Sometimes so loud it gives you a fright
He likes to play with his toys
He always makes a lot of noise
But he used to play on the grass
And run round and round very fast
A month ago he died at the vet's
And we still haven't forgotten him yet.

Louise Gilmour (10)
Rashielea Primary School

MY BROTHER

My brother once won an award
For being rather smart,
He also won another one for being good at art
He has quite a kind heart
Which makes me wonder why
How he grew at his age, to be rather high.

His eyes are blue
His shoes are black,
No wonder why he always has a sore back.
If he wasn't here right now,
I don't know what I would do,
I love him and I hope he loves me too.

Jane Turner (10)
Rashielea Primary School

I WANT . . .

I want a dog
I want a cat
I want a fish
No! No! No! No! No!
He wants everything.
Every time he sees something it's
I want! I want! I want!
So we tell him to go shopping
We give him a tenner
He eats all the sweets
And gets sick
Now we don't hear
I want! I want! I want!

Mark Melville (10)
Rashielea Primary School

HOLIDAYS

H   olidays are nice to have
O   nly I can't afford one
L   uggage you drag along
I   only wish I could go on holiday
D   ays and days go by
A   nd I wait and wait
Y   et I haven't been on holiday
S   urely soon I will be away.

Ashleigh McNair (10)
Rashielea Primary School

BLUE

Blue, the colour of the sky
The colour of my favourite team
Oh blue, won't you stay with me?
Blue's my favourite colour
The colour of the sea
Oh blue, won't you stay with me?

Scott Diamond (10)
Rashielea Primary School

CATS

C   ats see best in the night
A   courageous hunter
T   rees allow cats to climb them
S   ighing sadly cats die sooner than people do, goodbye.

David McFadyen (10)
Rashielea Primary School

MY PET SCOOBY

My pet Scooby was black
I played with him, he played with me
I loved him, he loved me
I slept beside him, he slept beside me
I walked with him, he walked with me
He kissed me, I kissed him back
I loved him very much
But now my pet Scooby is gone.

Dean Morell (10)
Rashielea Primary School

HOLIDAYS

Holidays are full of fun
I like playing in the sun
I like playing on the beach
To get a tan the colour of peach
But when it's over, I start to weep
I weep and weep until I'm asleep.

Jade McBride (10)
Rashielea Primary School

SCHOOL

S   chool is a surprise
C   ause I love a surprise
H   ow do surprises work?
O   h my favourite is a surprise
O   h my favourite is a surprise
L   ove at three fifteen, home time!

Samantha Shand (10)
Rashielea Primary School

BADMINTON

B adminton is my favourite sport
A square is the shape of the court
D own in the square, I play
M ainly we say 'Go get'm out!'
I n the gym, there is a court
N ow it gets hard.
T oo hard sometimes,
O n Mondays and Fridays I go
N ever do I miss a practise.

Hayley Morell (10)
Rashielea Primary School

SCHOOL

S chool is fun, school is great
C hildren all shapes and sizes, especially my mate
H olidays are fun too
O n Fridays it's assembly time for a few
O n the 13th February, we go on a trip
L ate afternoon at 2.15, on a Thursday
      I go to Miss Molloy.

Emma Bennett (10)
Rashielea Primary School

MY BED

B eds are nice and soft
E verybody should have a bed
D reams come when you are in bed.

Leigh Tennant (10)
Rashielea Primary School

HAMSTERS

H ide and seek is his game
A n all day animal is what he is
M umbling is what he does
S melling the fresh air in the morning
T easing him is what I do
E ating his fresh food
R olling about in the summer grass
S niffing about as he smells a cat nearby, hiss.

Heather Logan (10)
Rashielea Primary School

SURPRISING SCHOOL

S chool is full of surprises
C hildren of all shapes and sizes
H andwriting is my favourite subject
O utings are absolutely perfect
O h, I am amazed at what I've seen
L ove it, especially at 3.15!

Andrew Taylor (10)
Rashielea Primary School

MESSY HARRY

Harry my hamster throws his food everywhere
He puts it in his tunnel
He puts it in his house
When we clean his cage,
There is food everywhere!

Amy Bennet (8)
Rashielea Primary School

PAPERS EVERYWHERE

There's papers in the hall
And papers on the floor
There's papers on the wall
And papers on the cupboard door
Whenever Daddy's in the lounge
There's papers everywhere!

Nicole Reid (8)
Rashielea Primary School

THE MIAOWING KITTENS

'Miaow! Miaow!'
say the kittens
on a summer's night,
eating the cat food.

They sit in their basket
thinking that their ball
is an apple.

Rees McKechnie (8)
Rashielea Primary School

FOOD EVERYWHERE

There's burgers on the floor
Chips on the chair
There's sauce on the wall
And pudding on the ceiling
Whenever Scott eats his food
Food goes everywhere!

John Young (8)
Rashielea Primary School

FOOTBALL

F   ooty is my favourite sport,
O nly once a week does our pitch get used as a tennis court.
O val pitch, so it is
T oo muddy that I always miss
B ounce the ball and kick it out
A ll my friends shout 'What's this all about?'
L ike the game
L ove it too.

Nathan Shepherd (10)
Rashielea Primary School

WOOF! WOOF!

'Woof! Woof!'
say the dogs
on a rainy day.
They sit in their basket
thinking that sparkling stars
are an enchanted city.

Alicia McKenna (8)
Rashielea Primary School

FOOD EVERYWHERE

There's potato on the ceiling
And gravy on the chair.
There's a chicken on the floor
And on the door.
When Samantha has her lunch,
There's food everywhere!

Nicole McKinnell (8)
Rashielea Primary School

High School

H igh School is time to sigh
I   n school you should avoid trouble
G o home after a hard days work
H ome for a cup of tea.

S   eeing all the big people laugh and shout
C   rowd up and smashing about
H   igh school, when people dog
O   ver the top in a bog.
O   ut having fun, when teachers are demented
L   eaving school, what a hurry, out we come, what a scurry.

Adam Smith (10)
Rashielea Primary School

Messy Mum

There's potato on the ceiling
And carrot on the floor
There's roast beef on the wall
And peas in the bath
And chips in the sink
Whenever my mum eats
That's the state of the house.

Paul McCafferty (8)
Rashielea Primary School

Morven's Food

There's tomatoes on the ceiling
And pudding on the floor,
There's carrots on the chair
And gravy in her hair.

There's spaghetti on her hands
And potatoes on her arms.
Wherever Morven has her lunch
There's food everywhere!

Lauren MacKinnon (8)
Rashielea Primary School

SCHOOL

School is the best place ever
Not one person can hate school, never!
School is really quite fun,
In the playground, you see everyone run.
My teacher is really quite kind
My friend is Jane
At playtime, we play a game
Home time is the worst time ever.
That's the time when you think you'll
Never see school again, never!

Jessica Watkins (10)
Rashielea Primary School

THE SQUEAK, SQUEAK MICE

'Squeak! Squeak!'
Say the field mice on a hot summer's afternoon
When the crops are growing in the field.

'Squeak! Squeak!'
They sit in their giant long grass
Thinking what they will have for dinner.

Fraser Thompson (8)
Rashielea Primary School

MY FISHES

My fishes swim around the water
Like birds flying through the sky
Experts say they can't remember
As well as you and I.
My fish are lots of different sizes
From large to medium and small
But there's one that stands out from the rest
The biggest gold fish of them all.

Gareth Wilson (10)
Rashielea Primary School

GRASS EVERYWHERE

There's grass on the sofa,
There's grass on the carpet,
There's grass on the clothes
And grass on the wall
Wherever Adam plays football
There's grass everywhere!

Morgan O'Neill (8)
Rashielea Primary School

THE HISSING SNAKES

'Hisssss!' Say the snakes
On a sunny summer's day.
They sit in their wobbly branches
Thinking that the grass
Is waving farewell.

Megan Thomson (8)
Rashielea Primary School

DOGS

'Woof! Woof!'
say the dogs
on a cold winter's night
when children are outside having
a snowball fight.
'Bark! Bark!'
they sit on their doormat
thinking that their tails
are poisonous snakes.

Kevin Lee (8)
Rashielea Primary School

WHY MUMMY WHY?

Why are the trees green?
Why is the wind *never* seen?
Why is the grass low?
Do noisy people always live down below?
Why Mummy why?

Why do biscuits stick to your hips?
Why do clothes on a line need pegs?
Why are you always looking for curtains,
And always cleaning the sink?
I've really tried, but it's so hard to think.

Why Mummy why?
Why does Daddy hog the chair, the fire and the telly?
Why does Grandad have no hair,
But such a huge belly?
Why Mummy why?

Rachel-Anne Clarke (10)
St Mary's Primary School, Greenock

WHY DAD!

Why do people cry?
Why does Superman fly?
Why is the door always open Dad?
Why does my brother always lie?

Why does the phone ring?
Why does a trampoline have a spring?
Why did Mum marry you Dad?
Was it because of the beautiful ring?

Why should I not talk to a stranger?
Why did the Lord have to sleep in a manger?
Why is it my tea's always cold Dad?
Why do some signs say *Danger?*

Mark Hendry (10)
St Mary's Primary School, Greenock

I WISH I HAD THREE CATS

I wish I had three cats,
Who always sat on mats,
They would be so cute and furry,
And like the smell of curry.
When they start to play,
They'd jump around all day
And when they want to eat,
They'd curl round my feet.
When it's time for bed
I'd stroke them on the head,
And wish them all goodnight,
As they wrap up nice and tight.

Gill Loftus (11)
St Mary's Primary School, Greenock

WHY MUM?

Why is the sky blue?
Why is the grass green?
Why is the sun yellow?
Why is the dirt black?
Why mum why, are they all those colours?

Why are bugs small?
Why is sand so very small?
Why are pebbles so really small?
Why mum why, are these things small?

Where does the sun go when it goes down?
Where do puddles go when the sun comes out?
Where mum where do they go?

Why can I not fly?
Why can I not stay under water?
Why can I not jump very high?
Why mum why, can I not do these things?

Martin Turner (10)
St Mary's Primary School, Greenock

THE STORMY DAY

I am sitting in my classroom
I look out of the window
Cars were flipping over
Trees were shaking
Leaves were blowing fiercely
Flying umbrellas
I'm lucky
I'm inside.

Craig Walker (10)
St Mary's Primary School, Greenock

TREASURE UNDER THE SEA

There's a sparkle and a splash,
We're in the sea at last,
If there is treasure under here
I wonder where it could be?

Oh look a sunken ship!
Is there a monster in there?
There's the valuables lying in the mud,
I'm going to be very wealthy.

Let's take it to the shore,
It's too heavy to get it out of the pirate ship,
Silly me, it's tied to the ground,
I'll untie it, let's go up now.

I've opened the chest,
It's a luxurious sight.
With all this gold,
It's too good to be true.

All this fortune lying in the mud,
I wonder why no one found it?
It's probably been down here for a century or two,
It's the best riches ever to be found.

Helen McBride (11)
St Mary's Primary School, Greenock

OH TELL ME WHY DADDY?

Why is the snow white?
Why is the grass green?
Why is the sky blue?
Oh tell me why Daddy?

When can I walk?
When can I talk?
When can I fly?
Like a bird in the sky!

Gaynor Kincaid (10)
St Mary's Primary School, Greenock

WHERE IS THE TREASURE?

I wonder where the treasure is?
Maybe behind the attic door,
Or under a board in my bedroom floor,
I've been running around in circles
And now I'm in a tizz.

I've searched in every single room,
Including the cupboard under the stairs.
I cannot find it, it's just not there.
Or . . . maybe I'll ask the Man in the Moon.

I've searched in the garden, took lots of time,
All around the flower beds I've looked.
In the garden shed, in the pots of paint
Then carved in the garden wall, I found
A very secret sign.

I waved my hand across the wall,
In the blink of an eye, I was transported through time,
And my eyes were met with a sight so fine,
The treasure! I've found it!

Sara Downey (10)
St Mary's Primary School, Greenock

WHERE IS EVERYTHING

Where is my cat
Who smells like a rat?
Where is my dog
Who's as brown as a log?

Where is my parrot
Who like to eat carrots?
Where are my goats
Who doesn't like boats?

Where is my mum
Who likes to drum?
Where is my dad
Who's very mad?

Sean McDade (10)
St Mary's Primary School, Greenock

QUESTIONS!

Why do birds fly?
Why do dogs bark?
Why do children cry
In the dark?

What is space?
What is a race?
A bunch of stars
Or motor cars?

Oh why, why, why!
Are there so many questions to ask?
Why?

Gordon McDonald (10)
St Mary's Primary School, Greenock

STRAWBERRIES

A red strawberry I love so much,
A red strawberry I like to touch.

A purple strawberry isn't all that nice,
It kind of tastes like hairy, brown mice.

A red strawberry is full of juice,
I like it with creamy, white skoosh.

A purple strawberry I don't like to eat
Somehow it's just not like a piece of meat.

A red strawberry is a type of fruit
Somehow it doesn't look all that cute.

A purple strawberry you'll need to mend
Sometimes its life will come to an end!

Jennifer Dyer (10)
St Mary's Primary School, Greenock

THE HAUNTED HOUSE

What's that thing up on the hill
Is it true, it's got a bill?
Shall we take a closer look,
Will we take with us a book?
Our flashlight flashes, then go dead,
What's that I see? Is it a head?
I hear an *ooooh!* Is it a ghost?
Oh Emma please, please do not boast.
Do you want to go back to the haunted house,
And see if we can catch a mouse?
Okay, but let's go in for Jill.

Lyndsay Skilling (9)
St Mary's Primary School, Greenock

WHY?

Why do birds fly in the sky?
Why does the cat play with the rat?
Why does the phone ring a tone?
Why do people always chat?

Why does my sister always moan?
When she's chatting on the phone?
Why am I not allowed to moan?
When I am chatting on the phone?

Why do children go to school?
Is it so they can learn rules?
I think it's not fair,
When we have to sit in a chair.

Stephanie Bellingham (10)
St Mary's Primary School, Greenock

WHY?

Why is the sun yellow?
Why is the sun red?
When it goes down I like to go to bed.

When does it rise up?
When does it go down?
I really like that because it lights up the town.

Where does it go?
I'd like to know
It's really confusing me so.

Aidan Linning (10)
St Mary's Primary School, Greenock

THE QUESTION IS . . .

How do we live?
Why is the grass green?
How can we see, Dad?

Why is red called red?
Why do we have to work?
Why is the world round, Mum?

Why do kangaroos bounce?
Why is the sun so bright?
How do we grow, Dad?

Why is the snow so cold?
How do glasses make things bigger?
Why is Italy shaped like a boot, Mum?

Why oh why is everything why?

Jessica Beaton (10)
St Mary's Primary School, Greenock

HIDDEN TREASURE

Where is the hidden treasure?
In a box or in a bin?
I don't care because
My head is in a spin!

Is it beside my father's key?
Is it hidden up in a tree?
I don't know where it could possibly be.
When I find it
I'll be filled with glee!

Marc Dewar (10)
St Mary's Primary School, Greenock

WHERE ARE YOU?

Where are you Bill?
Are you on the tree?

Where are you Gill?
Why can't I see?

Where are you Ted?
Are you under the bed?

Where are you Tom?
Where have you gone?

Where are you everyone?

Boo!
I've found you!

Victoria Stevens (10)
St Mary's Primary School, Greenock

WHERE IS IT?

Where is my cat?
She's very fat.
Where is my dog?
He rolls like a log.
Where is my rabbit?
She has a bad habit.
Where is my fish?
He is in that dish.
Where is my rat?
He's been caught by the cat.

Amanda Campbell (10)
St Mary's Primary School, Greenock

MY BIKE

Every day I go on my bike
Riding down the hills with the wind in my hair
Put your gear into high
And you're ready to go.

I love to ride my bike
Go down the steepest hill
Go up the highest
Then press your pedals.

I love to ride my bike
Going in circles
Zigzags as well
Backwards and forwards.

I love to ride my bike.

Sean Nelis (10)
St Mary's Primary School, Greenock

WHY

Why can fish swim?
How can dogs walk but not talk?
Why can birds fly? Why can't I?
Why can I not be a dog, or a fish or even a bird?
When can I get a pet?

I sometimes look at the stars,
I even wish I was on Mars,
I always wish that I could catch a fish
The size of the whole world
Oh, how I wish!

Ryan Moran (9)
St Mary's Primary School, Greenock

THE DANCING TREE

On my way to school
I saw a tree dancing
Like people at a party
Waving their hands in the air.

I got into school
I looked out of the window
It was still dancing.

A fierce lightning came
It struck the poor tree
When I went out
There it was
Down on the ground
Never dancing again.

Jamie Hossack (10)
St Mary's Primary School, Greenock

WHY OH WHY?

What is the time?
Why do poems rhyme?
What is a sigh?
Why do I cry?
What is lightning?
And why is it frightening?
Why is it a pleasure
Having lots of treasure?
Mum,
Why oh why?

Sean Hughes (9)
St Mary's Primary School, Greenock

I WONDER

I wonder where you are?
Are you driving in a car?

I wonder where you're going?
The forecast says it's snowing.

I wonder where you're at?
The RSPCA buying a cat?

I wonder what you're wearing?
A coat, a jumper or more clothing?

I wonder what's the time?
Is it past nine?

Good night
Sleep tight
Let's turn off the light.

Kayleigh Wishart (11)
St Mary's Primary School, Greenock

BALLOON

Up, up and away we go,
Up so high
In the sky,
Feeling light
With the stars so bright,
Float past the moon,
So big and round,
Back to Earth
Without a sound.

Christopher Gillan (10)
St Mary's Primary School, Greenock

THE SILVER WOLF

The silver wolf, she stands alone,
Her coat like crystal, her eyes like stone.
The bitter, harsh winter is coming soon,
As she howls her loneliness under the full moon.

The moon is shining, an awesome light,
As the silver wolf howls with all her might!
Still the night goes on as does the silent suffering,
Of the silver wolf who has but nothing.

At last it is the time to mate,
Silver wolf hurries before it's too late,
Many years has she longed for a cub,
And now is her chance to make it up.

The moon's glorious, enchanting rays,
Reflect upon the silver wolf's gaze.
For now she has a family,
So she can live in peace and harmony.

The moon is shining, an awesome light,
As the silver wolf howls with all her might.
No longer is loneliness in the air,
But happiness, love and forever care.

Stuart McGowan (11)
St Mary's Primary School, Greenock

A SNOWY DAY

White day, flakes falling from the sky.
Chilly feet and cold hands,
Freezing, chittering, can't wait to get home,
Children out on sledges sledding down the street.

This is my favourite time of year,
With nice warm food inside me,
I put on all my cosy clothes,
Sitting by the fire keeping warm.

Lucy Rodger (10)
St Mary's Primary School, Greenock

ANIMALS

I like newborn kittens,
I like puppies too,
But what I like most of all
Are lion cubs in the zoo.

The budgie that my gran has
Is very, very cute,
But I like him most of all,
When he goes down his chute.

My cousin's baby rabbit,
Is only six weeks old,
When she wakes up in the morning
Her beautiful ears unfold.

I like newborn kittens,
I like puppies too,
But what I like most of all
Are lion cubs in the zoo.

My best friend's golden hamster
Has a very messy cage,
I'd better stop my poem now
Or I'll run right off the page!

Lauren Cummings (11)
St Mary's Primary School, Greenock

MY DAD, JOLLY OR SAD?

My dad's often called Rab,
He's sometimes jolly or sometimes sad.
He's running around looking mad,
My dad's often called Rab.

My dad's often called Rab,
He's sometimes jolly or sometimes sad.
He's running about, falling in and out,
My dad's often called Rab.

My dad's often called Rab,
He's sometimes jolly or sometimes sad.
You'll never spot him sitting on his bottom,
My dad's often called Rab.

Rebecca Dorrian (11)
St Mary's Primary School, Greenock

THE MONKEYS IN THE TREES

The monkeys were swinging in the trees,
Unlike people - you and me.

Monkeys are not like fish,
They only like the trees that swish.

Monkeys swinging left and right,
Oh, jumping out to give me a fright!

Monkeys never go to school,
They stay in the jungle - that's quite cool.

If you want to know what monkeys are,
They're not like humans, *they don't have a car*!

Gillian Alford (11)
St Mary's Primary School, Greenock

PIRATES

A pint of grog, a seafaring man,
A cutlass, a cannon, the Jolly Roger flying high,
A swashbuckling captain, a young cabin man,
The sails full power, the cook under the deck making a pie,
The Jolly Roger flying high.

Ship ahoy!
A ship closing in, their cannons are ready,
Prepare to attack, oncoming boarders,
The ship's not sailing, yet it stands very steady,
We defeated the boarders, hats off to you.

The hull has been punctured, we're taking on water,
Abandon the ship, launch the rowing boats.
So that seafaring man whom no one now knows,
With his bandanna and eyepatch was lost out at sea
Now sleeps on the seabed never to be defied.

Colin Wilkie (11)
St Mary's Primary School, Greenock

FISH

F   antastic, fabulous colours, all my pet fish
    have beautiful, wonderful mixed colours!
I   ndigo, blue, orange, red and green,
    all the colours of the rainbow and also of
    tropical exciting fish, swimming in the ocean.
S   peedy fish racing about in the pond, in and out
    of rocks, trees and seaweed.
H   andy for dentists and doctors too!

Gary McConnachie (11)
St Mary's Primary School, Greenock

THE YELLOW AND RED BANANAS

A red banana I've never seen,
Everyone says I'm as mad as I've always been.
Yellow bananas are the only kind,
A yellow banana is all you'll find.

A red banana I'll never eat,
A yellow banana is the kind you'll meet.
A red banana is red inside,
I don't want a banana with that inside.

A red banana I've never seen,
Everyone says I'm as mad as I've always been.
Yellow bananas are the only kind,
A yellow banana is all you'll find.

A red banana is red and ripe,
Just like a shiny red pipe.
A yellow banana is yellow and bright,
Just like the sun when it goes in at night.

A red banana I've never seen,
Everyone says I'm as mad as I've always been.
Yellow bananas are the only kind,
A yellow banana is all you'll find.

Jonathan Dyer (11)
St Mary's Primary School, Greenock

MY SILLY DOG TOBY

Toby is my little dog,
He's coming up for ten.
I did not want him to grow up,
When he was just a little pup.

When I took him for a walk,
I always had to run.
He pulled so hard it hurt,
But it was loads of fun.

He's black and white,
He howls at night.
And even though he does not bite,
I sometimes get an awful fright.

He runs away when he's bad,
And comes back very smelly.
We feed him food and he begs for more,
Until he's got a full belly.

But now he's old and grey and hairy,
All he does is sleep,
I love my dog,
Without him life would be bleak.

Kieran Millar (12)
St Mary's Primary School, Greenock